Answers 1

Exercises and Insights of a Masterful Life

Ivan Bava

OA

Answers from Within
Exercises and Insights of a Masterful Life
2nd improved edition

Author: Ivan Bava
Copyright © 2017 by Ivan Bavčević

Original title: Znanje je u Tebi
Originally published in 2017 by Poslovno savjetovanje OMNI, Croatia as per permission by Ivan Bavcevic

All rights reserved. Any part of this book cannot be reproduced in any form nor can it be copied, scanned or electronically adapted for public use, except for the short quotations in articles and magazines, without prior written authorisation of the publisher.

Publisher's note:
The author of this book does not give health advice nor does he prescribe usage of any particular technique as a form of treating physical or health problems without consulting a doctor. The author's intention is only to help the reader in searching for his/her emotional and spiritual wellbeing, since the emotional and spiritual wellbeing support physical health.

Dedicated to the Cosmic Source

Expression of Gratitude

I want to thank the Cosmic Mother and Father for the gift of this Knowledge. I want to thank my earthly parents Dušanka and Željko for the gift of life, and the care and love that they have given me. Special thanks go to Sri Sathya Sai, my beloved teacher and the embodiment of unconditional love and mercy without whom I would not be where I am now.

Thanks to all the teachers in all forms all these years, from my family and friends to strangers and colleagues, for pointing out to me the mistakes and hidden inner negativities, helping me in difficult situations, supporting me and sustaining me physically, materially and emotionally, and for loving me and enjoying with me the adventures of life.

Thanks to all the participants from my seminars and lectures without whom these thoughts would not have been said nor written down for the benefit of future readers. My thanks go to Sanja Tapušković who listened to the audio recordings of the seminars and transcribed some of the valuable parts that are in this book. Thanks to the whole team of The Center of Consciousness that made publishing this book possible.

As for the English version of this book, I am especially grateful to my beloved friend, mentor and guide, prof. Gladys Winkworth who has been like a guardian angel to me ever since I enrolled at the American College of Management and Technology in Dubrovnik, Croatia. She came to my rescue many times, including at the time of publishing this book. The English translation of this book was greatly assisted by Vanesa Stošić from Serbia who did the initial draft, and for this I am grateful.

Thanks to all of you who I cannot name in this moment, but who have left a deep mark on me, a mark of spiritual and psychological growth, of care and of love. The list of your names could extend for several pages and for that I am eternally grateful. You can be certain that I keep you in my heart!

Ivan Bavčević Bava, Split-Croatia, November 2019.

How to Read This Book

The basis of this book are the transcripts from the lectures that I gave in Croatia, Slovenia, Serbia and India from the year 2010 to mid 2013, that were later extended and enhanced by the suggested exercises and daily activities. The topics and texts in the book serve as a daily reminder or an answer when we have a certain question. The book is here. You can reach into it easily, or just open it randomly so that Life could guide you in the required situation. There are no coincidences, so feel why you have opened that particular text and message.

After every message you read, take a few minutes and contemplate it. The intellectual knowledge is not enough; it is important to feel the message from the inside, to awaken, integrate, apply, and allow it to become a part of you. Generally, you can close your eyes after every message, direct your attention to your breath, exhale the tension while feeling relaxation and observe what you're feeling and what is coming to you, what you must do. It is you speaking to yourself because the highest part of your Consciousness (the Higher Self) is sending the message to the mind and the earthly consciousness (the ego self) about what to do and how to move forward.

Let this book be your permanent life companion and a source of solutions in difficult situations.

You will notice that I often use the capitalised version of the word *Consciousness* throughout the text, which in that form is meant to represent the Eternal Level of Your Being, the Higher Self, or what I would call "The Real You".

Introduction

"I was gratified to be able to answer promptly, and I did. I said I didn't know." - Mark Twain

I have spent my adult life endeavouring to discover the way to access the power of consciousness and of the Creator in creating a happy and fulfilled life. In the summer of 2010, I became aware of the three keys of accessing the All-Knowing Source within us through the ALO method ("Allow, Let go, Hand Over and Surrender"), which was "downloaded" into my awareness in a moment of great spiritual clarity and vision. By admitting that at a conscious level I really do not know much, suddenly all the necessary knowledge at any moment was available and given by my inner guidance system, my inner compass. I realised that all along it was this intelligence of the universe that allowed me to travel through four continents and almost forty countries to work with some of the richest people on the planet, to set up my own companies, to lead several domestic and international associations with hundreds of members who change the world for the better, to hold lectures at universities, to advise businesspeople and corporations, to work with some of the greatest artists, singers, and dancers in world theaters, to live in harmony with the Creation, and to enjoy the maximum of life, love, and friends.

This book is a collection of messages that come from within us, from the inner compass that is the true intelligence of our life. In the beautiful freedom of not having to consciously know all the answers, you can be open to receive the most appropriate one for this exact moment. Hundreds of readers of this book in other languages have communicated to me saying that they have almost always opened the book at the most appropriate page in a given situation.

Consciousness, Life, and Feeling

"Your heart is the Light of this world. Do not cover it with your mind."
- Mooji

The Knowledge Is Within You

We did not come here to learn but to remember. We came here to feel ourselves.

What Does Life Want from Me?

Life wants you to feel the consequences of your choices. That is the only thing life expects from you. There are no rules, no special laws, and no good or bad. There is no recommendation for life because to life, it is all the same. It is all the same to life because all is one and the same. The only thing life expects from you is to feel the consequences of your choices. Any choice you make, you will feel the consequence. That is the way of life.

- Practice for the Day -

Pay attention to the consequences of your previous choices that you are living now. Notice what it was that you decided in the past which is present today as something pleasant or unpleasant. The decisions regarding what to study, what job to take, whom to live with, and where to move have far-reaching consequences on your present life. The power lies in the knowledge that you made those decisions (even if somebody forced you to, you decided to consent to their will). Link the consequences with the decision and conclude that today you can make a different decision. If you decided before, you can do it now too. You have the right to change your mind and create new consequences from your decisions.

Your Teacher

When you feel the consequences of your choices, you draw a conclusion about how to behave the next time. You conclude what is good for you and what is not. The experience and the feeling from the consequence are your teachers. However, if you run away from the consequences of your actions, your choices; if you postpone the consequences of your choices for tomorrow, for the day after tomorrow, for the next year, for the next life; what happens to you? Then you usually get born in a new body in another life and you bear the consequences of choices that you don't even remember. Then you feel like a victim because you cannot see why something is happening to you. So use this opportunity to recognise and feel the consequences of your choices from this life in this life.

A lot of things that happen to us don't have a visible reason in this life. It seems like we were born under an unlucky star. These are the situations we carried from one life to the other. If we consider that you most likely don't know how to travel through time and go back to the past, you can simply accept that there is a reason you are going through certain situations, and you should know that everything happens for your highest good. All difficult situations are only the way in which life cleanses the negativities from the past to bring things in balance. Maybe there is not much you can do about the past, but today you can choose to live in a way that will not create problems for the future. What ever life brings you, you can live it without resistance and fear, and know that it will never bring you anything that you cannot handle.

Do Not Postpone! Feel!

How do you postpone feeling the consequences of your choices?

You run away from the consequences and lie about things that you did or said. Many of us do it every day. You can run successfully, not dealing with anything, hiding the truth, twisting the facts, saying only the part of the truth, not wanting to have a conversation that you need to have, running away from a relationship, and running away from the responsibility for the words spoken and the deeds done. Those are the ways in which we postpone the consequences. We postpone feeling the consequences of our previous choices and decisions, although they will inevitably catch up with you.

Feeling is the key word here. The only thing life is asking of you is to feel the consequences of your choices. The problem is they will inevitably happen, but will you feel them or run away from that experience? The solution lies in feeling and living them.

- Practice for the Day -

What do you find difficult to admit? What are you not saying the whole truth about? What is that weight on your chest that is not allowing you to sleep? What is the wound hurting you? Gather your strength, and say it. Start by admitting it to yourself. Maybe you can speak to the sky, to the sea or to a forest. Maybe you will speak to the people involved. In any case, you will see how the truth sets you free and gives you peace of mind.

Notice the Mechanisms

When you feel the consequences of your choices, you can stop and ask yourself, "Does this choice serve me?" Your ego will say, "Oh, this pain; poor me; I am terrible; what have I done?" It will blame you your whole life so it can leave you in a low state of consciousness.

On the other hand, the spirit, or consciousness, will *feel* the consequence and say, "Oh, this is not for me." In the consciousness, there will be no mentioning of "how terrible I am; what have I done; poor me; I am guilty; whip me." In the consciousness, there is none of that. Consciousness just says, "I am not going to repeat this; I go on; Now I will be living differently." That is what the consciousness does. The consciousness feels and decides what to do next. The ego feels, gets depressed, blames itself and others for a life time.

- Practice for the Day -

Is there something you feel guilty or ashamed about? Is there something that is depressing you? Observe those actions from the past, and just accept that they are not worth the pain and guilt you are feeling now. Decide that you don't want to feel that way anymore and that, as a result of your decision, you will not do things that might put you in the same situation in the future. Let this pain be a good motivation for changing your behaviour.

Saint and Sinner

The only difference between a saint and a sinner is that the saint did not give up. If you would read biographies of some saints you would see that many of them had pretty wild, vivid, and interesting lives, full of non-conformity to social norms. A saint also makes mistakes, but does not identify him/herself with the mistakes or the lower part of human personality. In spite of the mistakes and harm done, a saint continues in full faith to seek the highest divine expression of themselves, to correct the mistake, and to identify with their Divine nature. A sinner identifies himself with the action, feels guilty and ashamed of the action, runs from the consequences of those actions, asks for forgiveness, and then repeats the same or similar action. Saints identify themselves with their Divine nature, feel responsible for the mistake, offer a way of retribution for the mistake, and make sure not to repeat it.

Remember Who You Are

If your ego is disappearing, what does it have to do with you? The ego and the mind might be crying. The ego and the mind might be blaming themselves. The ego and the mind might want you to stay on the low level of consciousness, in shame and guilt and in apathy and in fear. But that is not you. You always have the possibility and the opportunity to say, "This is not me!"

- Practice for the Day -

Sit in silence, close your eyes, observe your breath going through your nose with each soft inhale and exhale, and ask yourself, "Who am I?" Don't look for the answer, and don't think about it. Just ask the question, and let the answer come to you by itself. Let the answer show up without your effort or searching. Let it hit you as a glimpse of recognition. Just let it fall on you like a snowflake on the ground.

Awakened Consciousness

When the emotions, thoughts, memories, and traumas come to you, that is the time when you should stay awake and know that they are not real.

It is good to let them express themselves. It is good to feel them, to cry them out, or to let them overcome you. It is not good to repress them, deny them, or block them. Allow yourself to experience that sadness and those thoughts. Watch them, and let them pass. Everything has its end because nothing in this world is eternal. Situations and problems in life will go away in the same manner they came. Just stay awake and conscious that you are the one who is aware of all that, who is observing all of that, and who allows all that to pass.

- Practice for the Day -

How to stay awake in consciousness?
You will stay awake because you will understand that if you are aware of something, you are not it. If you are aware of some thoughts or emotions, then it is obvious that you are not those thoughts and emotions but the one who is aware of them. As you start to comprehend that those thoughts and emotions are just the objects of your awareness, you will begin to pay attention to yourself as a subject, the one who is observing all of it. You will not be trapped in thoughts and emotions and in that way you will be awake. Soon it will be more interesting for you to pay attention to yourself as an observer, instead of whatever it is that you are observing.

Ego or Consciousness?

You can either function on the basis of your ego or on the basis of the Consciousness. There is an easy way for you to see which modality you are in. If the ego is controlling you in this moment, then all your thoughts are directed to the past or to the future. Due to the thoughts that come from the past, we mostly experience emotions of sorrow and anger. We are sad and angry because something happened or did not happen the way we wanted it. When we have such emotions, it means that our ego has taken control over us and that it dwells in the past. The other option is that the ego is in the future, which brings the emotions of fear and worry. You are worried and concerned for something that will come or will not come, you are afraid of how it will turn out, how it will happen and will it happen at all. When such emotions are present, it means that ego is dominating and that it dwells in the future.

Consciousness lives in the present moment and it is aware of what is present now inside of you and outside of you. It will allow all emotions, those based in the past and those caused by thoughts of the future, to flow through the body now, but it will not analyse them, judge them, or criticise them. It will not deny, change, ease, prevent, or dramatise them. It will not go into deeper thinking and repetition of images that intensify already present emotions. Consciousness will know that if it is aware of something then it is not it and it will let that situation or mood pass and release its energy. It will know that there will be a book, a method, a friend or a therapist who will be able to help you let go of all that controls you.

- *Practice for the Day* -

Become aware of where you spend most of your time. Is it in the past, present, or the future? Pay attention to the thoughts and emotions that prevail in your body and mind, they will give you the answer. After that you will have the chance to decide where you wish to stay from then on.

When the Light Turns on...

Be aware that when the light turns on, the dirt is clearly visible. Don't let it surprise you. Consciousness will shed light on all the unnecessary and redundant thoughts and emotions, on all the garbage scattered inside your being. Don't give up, don't draw back, let it not depress you because all of that was already there anyway. The fact that you don't see the garbage does not mean it is not there. When you turn on the light, it does not mean that the garbage appeared in that moment. It has been there all along. The difference is that you are going to clean it now; you will know it is not yours, that it is not you. You will ask yourself what is that garbage in your house, and then you will throw everything out. Do not be surprised by the first shock. The more you get shocked, the more you will yearn to clean everything as soon as possible. As the light gets stronger, it will seem as if it is harder for you than before, but actually it isn't. You have the support of Consciousness and now everything under its light will be cleansed.

All the garbage is contained in the personal identity, or the ego. Consciousness, the real You, is eternally pure like the cinema screen. No matter what film is being shown, the screen is always white and untainted by the film. In the same way, you are, as Consciousness, always pristine regardless of what is happening to the personal identity that bears your name. When you discover the negativities connected by your ego to your personality, and your character, don't get depressed, sad, ashamed or scared. It is not you! Dive in that garbage, scratch it, and dig it out. There should be no fear because you are not digging through yourself; you are digging through the personality that needs to perfect itself. When life sends you a situation, a partner, a lover, a colleague, a teacher, a therapist or a healer, let them dig out and throw out on the surface what lies in your psyche. Open up and surrender because they are not affecting you, they are removing that mask taken on by the ego.

The Path of Awareness

Consciousness is the light that will illuminate ignorance and remove the dust covering our spiritual essence. The path of spiritual awareness is not a technique. We can practice different healing, meditational, emotional, or self-help techniques our whole life, but it does not mean that we will be more spiritually aware, that we will be better people or that we will live by some higher spiritual values. Almost every energy or spiritual technique can be used as a tool to become conscious, but there are not many people using them in that way. Generally we heal our bodies and emotions or use techniques to have a better financial or love situation. Eventually, we get sick again, or experience the same situation, and get stuck in a spinning wheel of problem-solution.

The path of spiritual awareness is the way of living in order to stay awake and be aware of our eternal reality in every situation, while at the same time being aware of the events in this temporary physical appearance. It is the awareness that you are the actor, not the role that you are playing on the stage of life. You are the actor aware of yourself and aware of your role at the same time, and never forgetting who you really are.

Mind or Spirit?

At some point it happens that ego prevails. The mind prevails and says, "I am awful." This is how ego and mind speak. They will say, "Look at all of my mistakes throughout life, I did nothing for all those years; I always make errors; I am good at nothing; there is no help for me." After those words usually starts self-blame and shame for what you did, and that is the bottom of consciousness. Your mind and ego will always keep you at the lower states of consciousness; like sorrow, guilt, apathy and shame. That is not the way to spiritual awakening! On the other side, what will Consciousness do? Consciousness will see all that garbage, maybe get a bit unpleasantly surprised at the first moment, but it will not fall into shame or guilt, it will not give up. It will say to itself, "Now I see that things cannot be done in that way. What will I do now to live differently?"

You Are an Inexhaustible Source of Energy

It is a fact that you have access to unlimited energy. The question is do you live at the level of consciousness where you create infinite energy or do you live in the mind that thinks that there is not enough. Although it is true that you are a source and that energy is limitless, when you live your life in the mental concept which says that there is not enough and that you need to work real hard in order to earn something, then the mind which lives with the idea of poverty affects absolutely everything and can even turn the truth into a lie.

Therefore, the truth that you are a limitless source of energy could not manifest itself in your life because of the mental belief of limitation and insufficiency. Since the mind is the basis of this manifested universe, and it is at the same time the basis of that energy, if there is a belief in your mind that there is not enough, then that belief manifests itself in your life as such.

- Practice for the Day -

In which part of your life do you think that there is not enough and that you cannot? Where do you say the lie about limitation and insufficiency? Become aware of the lies that you say, such as: It is expensive; I don't have it so I can't give to you; It is not enough; I can't afford that; and so on. At least stop saying them, if you can't say the opposite. The truth could be something like: It is not expensive, but I have another priority now; I have, but not for that; I could give to you, but I don't want to; I always have everything I need.

Feel It in Your Heart. Stay in Your Heart.

As a human being you were created to be a Divine magnificent being. A **magnificent** being.

Know this truth, hear it: I come from magnificence; I attract magnificence in my life; I am magnificence. I come from abundance; I was born from abundance; I was created from abundance because I am abundance. If I was created from abundance, if I come from abundance, how can I be anything else but abundance?

Feel this truth in your heart: I come from the inexhaustible source of energy. I am the inexhaustible source of energy.

Body

"There is more wisdom in your body than in your deepest philosophy."
- Friedrich Nietzsche

Listen to Your Body

Through your body your Consciousness is telling you what it is that should not be a part of your life and what is not for you. It is simple - just listen to it!

- Practice for the Day -

Whenever you notice pain, discomfort, a spasm, contraction or sickness in the body, just sit in silence, focus on the part of the body that is attracting your attention and talk to it as if you were talking to another human being. Tell it, "Hi ... I see you. I allow you to exist." Exhale with relaxation and stay focused on that conversation. Ask that pain or organ, "What do you want to tell me? Forgive me for ignoring you before, now I am listening to you." Observe which is the first thought or feeling that comes to you, for that is your answer. Accept what the body is telling you and then do what it is asking of you. You already know it, it's just that you didn't want to admit it to yourself.

Relax the Body

Consciousness flows and goes only through a relaxed body. Stiff body is a sign that we are being in the lower, limited state of consciousness. Energy, Consciousness and Life all flow through a relaxed body. You flow.

- Practice for the Day -

Every day consciously and intentionally relax your body for 15 minutes. Lie on the sofa, bed or the floor, with the legs and arms not crossed, inhale deeply with relaxation a few times, and scan your body from the tips of the toes to the top of the head. As you go through your body with your awareness, it will relax. Then focus on the center of your chest and breathe into the center of the chest counting up to three and exhale counting up to five, letting all the tension flow down your body and out through the feet. Stay like that breathing and releasing tension for fifteen minutes.

Pure Physics - Body Posture Is the Key

Human body is an energy device through which the electrical, heat and energy in different shapes flows. The way we hold our body, the body posture, determines the energy flow of the body.

With bent shoulders, bowed head and a crooked spine you will have a big difficulty feeling brave and self-confident. **Straighten up!**

Always sit on the chair with a straight spine. While you sit on the chair don't cross your legs, don't put one leg over the knee of the other, but keep both feet on the floor. Walk straight with your head up and your chest and shoulders open.

Always be aware of your breath flowing in and out of the body.

What Is Your Body Showing?

Your body shows all your beliefs, all your opinions, all your experiences, all that has happened, all memories, all feelings and everything that you, as an individual being, lived from the beginning till today. Your body tells everything about you. The moment you change some of those components, a certain attitude, belief or a thought; when you erase some memory, then the physical appearance of the body will change too. In the same way, physical influences on your body will change mental attitudes and thinking.

- Practice for the Day -

You can start from both sides. Start mentally changing your beliefs and thoughts while at the same time you are changing the way you sit, walk or use your body. Work out, do a sport actively and use your muscles so that the blocked emotions would be released during the training.

Body-Mind Unit

Mind and body are linked processes that are both mental and physical at the same time. Body is the material form of the mind. Mind is the mental form of the body. Body is not in the process; body is the process; it is an event. We have to get used to the fact that the body is not an object, but an event which is in a constant flow and that there is not a second when the body is one and the same. Accept that the cells are changing constantly and that every thought causes the body to create an emotion, positive or negative.

- Practice for the Day -

Become aware of how your body reacts to the psychological states. Does your mind affect your heartbeat, the depth of breath, gastric juices or the activity of the intestines? Do you feel your liver or your spleen? Do you get diarrhoea from stress and fear? All this is telling you how your body is the direct consequence of the mind. Your body in the material world reflects what is happening in the energetic mental world of the mind.

What Is My Body Telling Me?

The body will always tell you what is happening with your whole being. When you observe your body it becomes clear to you which mental processes are harmful and which are good for you. The moment you become aware of that, Consciousness takes over the lead and the body returns back to balance. Consciousness returns the body to balance. The mind can thrill the body and send it very high, but that does not signify balance because it can also put the body down. The body is inseparable from the mind and hence has a reaction in order to show you, the Consciousness, that whatever the mind is doing now does not serve your life, does not serve your direction, and that you need to change your mental process or simply get away from it.

- Practice for the Day -

Chemical reactions in the body create emotions, and emotions are the easiest to be seen, there is no way you cannot notice them. You can go without noticing hidden beliefs. You can also miss noticing your attitudes sometimes because they are the deepest manipulators. But you cannot ignore the emotions and for that you should be grateful, because they show what is hidden and buried, and they are giving you the chance to free yourself of it.

Dance, Run, Jump!

The mind is limited and finite by its nature and for that reason it wants to make everything finite and static, like a painting. Consciousness does not have that need. It wants to move everything, liven up, make it fresh and actual, spontaneous and momentary. That is why the movement of the body is important, because moving takes us away from the mind that is static. When we get the body moving, we are in harmony with life.

- Practice for the Day -

Make room for moving your body in your daily routine. Urgently, if you haven't done it already, start jumping, running and dancing every day. Just like you sleep, eat, have a shower, go to the toilet and brush your teeth, you should also run, jump or dance for a few minutes every day. Don't trust me, trust your experience after a few days of such activity.

Enjoy Your Body

We have a body so that we could have all the experiences that we ever wanted, yet we keep running away from it to our thoughts, worries and plans. And then, when the life passes, we say, "Well, there goes my life!" Why do we need a body if we are going to run away from it and out of it? Don't run away from your body to your thoughts; don't try to leave your body as soon as possible because life in this body is what we wanted. We will enjoy all the other levels of existence as well, but let us now enjoy our bodies.

- Practice for the Day -

Suggestions for simple enjoyment in the body:
- *breathe in and then while you exhale gently make the sound: Haaaaaaa ...*
- *hug yourself, embrace yourself and stay like that for awhile*
- *go through your hair with your fingers*
- *gently touch your skin with the tips of your fingers and caress your neck, chest, stomach, arms, groin and legs*
- *gently touch your genitals*
- *stretch like a cat and roll over on your bed*
- *get a massage*
- *make a warm bath with salt and essential oils (for aura cleansing put 3 kilos of coarse sea salt and one litre of white wine vinegar in the tub, and lie in the hot water for 20-30 minutes)*
- *massage your feet while you are sitting, reading or watching a film*
- *lie on the sea surface and just float*
- *sunbathe on the hot sand or pebbles*
- *close your eyes while you chew food so you can feel all the tastes in your mouth.*

After you learn enjoying your body on your own, do all of this as a couple or mutually in a group.

The Spirit and the Heart

"Where the Heart is speaking, it is not polite for the Reason to put its own remarks."
- Milan Kundera

Meditation Brings Good Health

When we meditate, in a state without thoughts, the body heals itself because when there are no thoughts, nothing affects the body. When there are no thoughts, the mind does not exist because the mind is a set of thoughts. When the mind is on a break, Consciousness finally has a chance to express itself through the body. Consciousness only brings good health, it cannot bring sickness. The mind is the one bringing sickness.

- Practice for the Day -

Meditation in a few steps:
- *sit on a sofa or in a chair*
- *cross your feet and intertwine the fingers of one hand with another so that your palms lie relaxed in your lap facing up*
- *close your eyes*
- *take several deep breaths and exhale with relaxation*
- *relax your face, eyes, shoulders and spine. (You don't need to worry about keeping your spine straight.)*
- *observe your breath going through your nose with each gentle inhale and exhale*
- *don't control your breath, just observe it flowing without your effort. (Focus completely on your nose and breath and flow together with it.)*
- *if thoughts occur, go back to your breath as many times as you need to*
- *stay like that observing your breath in the state without thoughts for at least 20 minutes. Ideally you should be meditating each day as many minutes as is your age. If you are 40 years old, then 40 minutes of meditation.*

Conscious Observing

Affirm within yourself the following: "My mind and body are surrendered to the river of life, are surrendered to Me, to the Consciousness. My ego and mind accept everything that comes from the Source, from the Heart, and I neutrally observe everything as if it were a white screen where the film of the mind is projected. I am untainted by the mind. I observe. I am observing my mind, ego, emotions, thoughts and pain in the body. I observe ups and downs, joys and sorrows. I observe consciously. I am here and now, and my body is relaxed. My mind is surrendered to the Consciousness, and my ego accepts everything that comes and everything that is happening.

Free Flow of Energy

On the level higher than the physical, all of creation continuously makes love to itself. All beings are in continual exchange of energy. Allowing this free flow brings the state of purity. When we allow it to flow freely and unrestrained, life takes care of everything. Something happens, some person, some process, some healing, some insight, something comes that will put you in the state of purity. And you don't have to force anything. Energy itself changes the course. Consciousness does its own thing, when you finally let it flow.

- Practice for the Day -

Every day you can liberate the energy flow within a minute or two by relaxing the muscles and your whole body with deep inhaling and relaxed exhaling with the easy sound of "... Haaaa..." This can be done on top of a regular meditation that requires you to sit down for longer time and observe the breath.

Playfulness

Stop thinking of the concepts about life and spirituality as something very serious. Do everything you can to be playful, not to take anything tragically, not to experience resentment. We were born to be joyful, as children, playful and limitless. Then the society and family conditioned and directed us to hold on to negative thoughts all the time, thoughts based on fear, hunger, wars, poverty, incapacity, on crisis, loans and high mortgages. When we live in fear, we are easily manipulated. Become aware of the manipulation. Free and joyous people cannot be controlled.

- Practice for the Day -

You can start to be playful by going to a park and sitting on a swing, by walking on a rope or slack line, by playing board games, jumping on a trampoline, jumping into the sea, playing in the shallow sandy waters, playing with a beach ball, screaming and dancing with your friends, doing handstands, doing rolls forwards and backwards in a field, wearing costumes, organising masquerades, going down a zip line; The possibilities are endless.

Awareness of Breath and Awareness of the Heart

When you notice that you are being manipulated by the negative thoughts; when you stop in a moment and notice that anger or sorrow, misery or despair started overwhelming you; or that you feel like a victim; that means that you became overpowered by negative thoughts and emotions based on fear. Then you have the possibility to say, "I don't need this; what do I choose now?" And then you can replace those negative thoughts with some other thoughts. You can do that; you have that possibility in every moment.

To achieve this you always have access to simple and useful tools: meditation, awareness of your breath, awareness of where you are, and who you are, and awareness of the heart. Observe and just notice. Awareness of the heart and awareness of your breath make you present, allowing you to not fall into those ego traps, to be in the Moment.

- Practice for the Day -

Simply put your palms at the center of your chest. Close your eyes and focus your attention there. Several times take a deep breath and exhale with relaxation. Be completely aware of just your breath and the Heart Center in your chest. Stay like that until your body becomes completely overwhelmed with peace that springs from the Heart.

Start Today

You are not your mind and you are not from your mind. The mind is yours, you are not his or hers. You are not emotions; You are not personal attachments; You are not attitudes; You are none of that. In reality you are a spontaneous being who does not think in a particular moment what would a proper conduct be. In reality you are spontaneous and you do not react from the emotional level. You act spontaneously from the impulse in your chest. But how can you bring yourself to that real state if you continually react on the basis of crazy thoughts, emotions, memories, relationships, other people, past, traumas, laws of the society, education, TV or expectations? In that case you can't.

- Practice for the Day -

So start today. Decide and abandon everything that is not you and that is not yours. As soon as it comes to the surface, focus on the Heart and then with an exhale release that which you don't need. Without analysing, without hesitation and without resisting, let yourself feel that pain and emotion that is coming out, and then live it and exhale it. Release it then and there. Leave it there, at that place where it appeared. Exhale, relax your chest, relax the muscles and relax your body, as many times as you feel you need to.

The Hardest Addiction

In the book Journey to Ixtlan by Carlos Castaneda, the teacher says, **"I** have no routines or personal history. One day I found out that they were no longer necessary for me and, like drinking, I dropped them." Our own past – that is one of the main things that can die and it would be good that it dies. The attachment to our own past can die.

- Practice for the Day -

Become aware of which stories you keep repeating, what are you proud of or for which things you keep finding excuses or asking for compassion. Those stories from your past just keep the same vibration of your life. They hold the false picture about you and your life. You don't need that! When you become aware of the negative stories that you often repeat, then make a decision to stop yourself when you hear yourself telling them. Even if you are in the middle of a sentence, you can stop and say that it is not important because it is no longer true, because it is no longer you. As the great European river Danube has that name for many centuries, even though it is not the same water that used to run before (even not the same water from an hour ago), so you too have the same name although you are not the person you used to be a few years ago (even the person you were an hour ago).

Training Your Consciousness

You need to train your consciousness to be stronger than the mind. You cannot train your mind as long as you are weaker than it is. You can only be better than it is. However, when you don't know who you are, and you think that you are the mind or the body, or you think that you need to fight or constantly control it, you will not succeed; you will always fail. Just be aware. The training of your consciousness will make you better than the mind, which is, at the moment, a better player than many.

- Practice for the Day -

First train your consciousness in some easy situations, so that you are aware of yourself and everything that is going on while the situation is peaceful and pleasant; while you are cooking or driving a car; while you are reading a book, having a bath or sunbathing. Then start training in some more difficult situations while you are at work or in some duty. Just be aware of yourself as an observer and be aware of everything that is happening to you in your emotions and your thoughts. As soon as you notice tension or discomfort, breathe it out from your chest and relax the heart. Eventually you will be able to train with your parents, your partner and other sources of authorities or discomfort.

The Strength of Consciousness

Let's notice how far we are from the mastery of our own being. We will not accomplish that mastery forcefully, but by strengthening our Awareness. When your awareness becomes stronger, Consciousness takes over control by itself. It does not want to weaken the mind and the body. Consciousness wants a strong body and a strong mind, because it knows that the stronger and more powerful the mind is, the stronger the manifestation of its ideas and desires in physical reality is. Consciousness will never try to annul the mind that keeps this world in existence. Consciousness wants the mind to be strong, but it wants to be stronger than it, and not vice versa.

- Practice for the Day -

How much time per day do you spend only in being, in existing without thinking? Every mental process, each thinking, each imagining, only makes the mind stronger. Consciousness is strengthened with being without acting and thinking. Take time for yourself every day just to be, without doing anything, just look at the ceiling or the sky without looking at anything in particular. Immerse in the distance and just be.

Now is the right time! Put away this book and stay with yourself without anything. Let your eyes look anywhere, and let your attention withdraw into the heart.

Mastery Over the Mind

When the Consciousness prevails, when it gets back its own influence over the mind which was created by the Consciousness in the first place; then we will be able to manipulate the basic elements of nature with the help of the mind. It does not work in the opposite way. That is the reason why we will not give up our own mind, we will not destroy our mind, we will just become aware who is the boss and who is the servant there. Who created whom, who is directing whom.

The mind is a real expert because it practices 24 hours per day, 365 days per year. Even when we sleep, the mind practices. While we are allegedly resting, it keeps practicing. Unlike the mind, we rarely practice our awareness, our presence. And then we wonder how we become overpowered, manipulated and tired by our mind. Mind is like a first league football club, and presently we are somewhere in the third league. The mind trains all days in the week, and we remember to meditate maybe once a week. The mind trains 24 hours per day, and we think that practicing awareness for 20 minutes per day is enough.

- Practice for the Day -

If you want to be better than the mind, which was created to serve you, it is time to start practicing your awareness and presence every day. In this book there is advice on how to meditate, observe, and be awake and unattached to what is happening around you. All these are practices of awareness. Choose one of these practices and allocate 10min, 20min, 30min to that practice. How much time will you give to strengthening your consciousness.

Who am I?

"I am you, you are Me. You are a wave, I am the Ocean. Know this and be free, be Divine."
- Sathya Sai Baba

We Are Waiting for Your Gift

Consciousness expresses itself through different ways. You will have to discover by yourself which is your way. Are you pure love; Are you righteousness; Are you joy; Or are you a warrior? Are you silence? What are you, which is your expression of consciousness? If you are a warrior, be the best warrior. If you are love, be the biggest love. If you are peace, be the deepest peace. If you are dance, be the freest dance. If you are speech, be the best speech. What are you? Who are you?

- Practice for the Day -

I ask you to close your eyes and admit to yourself what it is that you are dreaming of from the beginning. See yourself in that. Don't think if it is possible now or not. Don't think about practical steps, finances and the realisation of the project. Allow yourself to acknowledge your dream, your love. Allow yourself to feel your heart pulsating when you see yourself while you do or live that, that which you have been negating and delaying for years. For now it is enough to admit that dream to yourself and allow it to be possible, even if you don't know how.

When I See You, I See Myself

When I speak to you, I speak to myself. When I look at you, I look at myself. When I listen to you, I listen to myself. When I touch you, I touch myself. When I smell the rose, I smell myself. When I taste the food, I taste myself. Everything I see is the reflection of the core essence of my being. Everything that I look at, I am looking at myself. Everything I see is me. Absolutely everything. And not just metaphorically, not just spiritually, not just in cosmic proportions, but practically, in every day situations.

- Practice for the Day -

Spend a day observing people, animals, areas, places and plants that surround you. Find some segment and reflection of yourself in everybody that you meet or see. It is life bringing you the mirrors so that you can see yourself and stop living in delusion. Only when you see yourself, can you decide to be different.

Everything I See - I See Myself

When you feel like a victim of somebody's behaviour, conditions or laws, then you cannot do anything. When you feel like a victim, you feel paralysed. Somebody else is guilty, I cannot do anything about that and I have to suffer. Then the despair and the feeling of powerlessness, misery, anger and frustration gets stronger. Feeling like a victim is the negation of your divine nature and it kills your power.

- Practice for the Day -

You should know that the problem is never, never, never, never in somebody or something else. That something is just a reflection of yourself. It is the most wonderful, the most direct message that you can get. Everything you see is you. See yourself in everything, in every object. Listen to what people in your life are telling you. Accept the message from the newspaper or from the radio. Listen to the sentence that was said on the street by a passerby. Look at the neighbours that surround you. Listen to the quarrels that you hear in your company. Discover yourself in everything, in everybody.

What you can do on your path of awareness is to become aware and say to yourself, "All of this is just a reflection of my consciousness and my psyche. Everything I see is myself." And then notice what Life is pointing at and where it is guiding you. Through those reflections Life will send you clear signs about your psyche that you need to heal so that it would be easier to walk through life.

The Mirror

Everything that you hold against somebody, look for and notice it in yourself. Heal it in yourself. If you resent it; if it makes you angry or upset; you should know that it is inside of you.

When the ego sees in someone else its own characteristics that it is trying to hide, then it simply goes mad and gets angry. If the ego overwhelms you, you will immediately point a finger at someone to blame, not realising that the other three fingers of your hand are pointing back at you. That will be a good sign that it is time to bring to light those characteristics of your personality which ego was trying to hide. Don't worry, it is just your personality, it is not you. Feel free to show it clearly; let the truth and honesty dissolve it.

Problem And Solution

As much as some situations in life seem to be somebody else's fault, as much as you might have concrete and material evidence, you should know that the cause and the solution lies in you. The program of virtual reality that is prevailing at the moment in the world is looking for the problem, for the cause, and for the solution in others and outside of you. Do not believe it, it is not anywhere else. Despite all the material, physical, written and other evidence, never, and I mean never, is someone else the real cause of the problem instead of you. And never, as much as it seems that it is, and as much you are convinced in your belief, will you resolve things in your life only by asking others to change something. Everything is always inside your mind and heart, in your psyche, your past, your family inheritance and your genes.

- Practice for the Day -

What you see in others is actually like an unpleasant thorn stuck deep in your heart and it hurts too much for you to even look at it. That has been lying there most likely since the childhood. Look inside, allow yourself to feel that pain and to see for how long it has been there. Who was the person who you believe limited you for the first time, punished you, scared you, lied to you or showed a negative habit? When you see that, let life bring you help and the solution through a therapist, a seminar or some other event that will spontaneously show up in your life.

The One Who Looks Inside Herself/Himself, Will Part from Himself/Herself

You cannot comprehend yourself by thinking. You can only go through Hell and meet the devil that is inside your mind. He is not outside of you. When you see him, you will wish to part from him. That devil will be something that you thought until now is actually you. That will be the ending of that idea about yourself, the end of your identification with your false self.

- Practice for the Day -

For the meeting with the Devil I suggest going away into solitude for a few days without any contact with other people, with civilisation, books, writing, prayers, TV, music, food or with any other of the stimulants with which we hide the rot which has accumulated inside of us. In that solitude, when the mind stays without something to do, when the suppressed emotions are no longer hidden by food; the crucial meeting between You and the inner terrorist which is stealing your life for years pretending to be You will happen. That is the moment when you will need to decide that you are ready to throw away everything negative existing inside, and to decide that you are no longer going to live by the direction of that voice or those habits. Then turn to Life and let it bring you the solution and the healing through some process, a person, a therapist, a situation or an event. If you don't know how to heal yourself, let Life show you how.

First Step

Don't go around solving things that are happening in the world, at least not as the first step. The first step would be to notice where in your life you are doing that same thing to other people and to yourself. Everything that you notice in the world is in fact in your consciousness, you wouldn't notice it if it wasn't. Become aware where you act in the same way towards close people or strangers, and most importantly, where and when you behave towards yourself in that way. You will surely find it. Heal yourself within and choose to behave differently in that regard. If that keeps existing in the world after your change, then you can decide what you will do about it. But firstly change it inside of you, before you go changing it outside of you.

Everything Is Inside of You, You Are Everything

Everything that you see is yourself. Your country is the reflection of yourself, the politicians are the reflection of yourself, the way the banks are, the way we import or treat food production, the corruption in our society, it is all you. The whole planet is the reflection of yourself. Each continent can relate to one of your chakras. Seven continents – seven physical chakras. What is Asia, Europe, Africa, America? Discover the answer. Each country can also relate to one of your chakras. Afghanistan and Iraq are inside of you. Where is the war within you? The highest country in the world, Tibet, is inside of you. The highest country represents the crown chakra, which is Consciousness. And who took the possession over it? Another country that represents the element of metal, that is the mental (mind), occupied the Consciousness. The mind actually occupied Consciousness. Is that not the truth about your life as well? Is that not how it generally is on the planet Earth right now?

Transformation

The transformation of this planet will not just happen by itself, but through human hearts, human bodies, and through the awakening of the individuals. It will not happen by waiting for somebody from outer space to bring it to us. In fact, that awakened state is already here. We just do not live it, because at the moment we live the lower frequency of consciousness. Therefore, we do not need to wait for it because it is already here, it is already true. We will finally become aware and have the experience of the high frequency, the high level.

- Practice for the Day -

Say to yourself, "I am opening myself to the experience of spiritual wakefulness. I am ready for the transformation and to let Life orchestrate all the events, people, situations and circumstances, so that, through my body, emotions, mind and heart, the transformation of life on Earth could become manifest."

My Truth

I deserve everything. I deserve all the best. That is my right and my truth. I come from the magnificence; I accept the magnificence in life; I am the magnificence. The place that I come from is Divine abundance. Born from the abundance, I was created from the abundance. That is the truth. That means that I am the abundance. If I was created from the abundance, how could I be something else? I come from silence, from peace, from love. I attract all of that into my life, because that is what I am, that is the truth. There is no modesty in the truth. It is magnificent. I do not create it neither bigger nor smaller than it is, I do not try to magnify it or minimise it. I just allow it to be big as it is.

- Practice for the Day -

Relax, breathe consciously and repeat to yourself the above text a few times, but with a feeling. Feel what it is like in your heart when you say to yourself, "I deserve all the best." Repeat as many times as you need to, gently and without force. Be patient with yourself. Feel every sentence on its own and let them integrate into your consciousness.

The Magnificent Life

Let everything magnificent come into your life. Not because the ego has that notion, but because you were born from the magnificence, so therefore you are the magnificence. Neither more nor less, just that. It is not necessary to think how much that is. In that case it would be a mental process that makes everything either bigger and destroys it or makes it smaller, and then says, "I am a nobody, who am I to be something like that?"

- Practice for the Day -

Say this to yourself, "I let the magnificence of life reveal itself to me in my own experience. I allow myself to comprehend my own beauty and value. I am opening myself to the experience of my magnificence."

Who Am I in This World?

I am not the one I thought I was. I cannot think about myself. I can only perceive myself. I am the one who is aware of the thinking; and thinking is always based on objects and things outside itself. I was often trying to think about myself; but I was actually only thinking about my behaviour, about my emotions, about my thoughts and memories, about my decisions and mistakes. When something is **mine** then it is an object I posses. I am the one who has behaviours, emotions, thoughts, memories, decisions and mistakes like I have clothes, a car, a house, a mobile phone or a laptop. So who am **I** that has all of that?

In this world, I come from Magnificence, I accept magnificence in my life, I am magnificence. I come from the inexhaustible source of energy; hence I am the inexhaustible source of energy. I come from the Divine; hence I am Divine. Nothing less and nothing more. Neither less nor more. Just that.

Embodied Consciousness

I was born from something big. I come from abundance. I truly come from abundance. I come from the strength, from power and energy. I come from all of that, I was created from that so I must be that. Ice is made of water, although it does not look like water. In the same way as ice is water in a different aggregate state, so am I Consciousness on Earth in another aggregate form.

The Spirit that pervades every particle of every atom of this universe only changes its density of existence. If we would compare the spirit (Consciousness) with milk, then our energy bodies (with thoughts and emotions) would be like yoghurt, and our physical body like cheese. All of that is milk, but in a different density of existence. All is spirit, in different density of materialisation.

Mind and Thoughts

"We are shaped by our thoughts; we become what we think. When the mind is pure, joy follows it like a shadow that never leaves."
- Buddha

Mind Is a Tool of the Creator

Sathya Sai Baba once said that human mind is the strongest instrument and tool that a man could have. He said that after the Consciousness there is nothing stronger in the universe. Mind is a tool with which Consciousness created the Universe. Mind is actually the basis of the Universe, so you can imagine how powerful that tool is. That is a device that Consciousness uses in order to create. Consciousness creates through the mind.

Why Does This World Seem Painful?

Most of the spiritual teachers refer to the mind as a monkey mind because it goes crazy. The mind is the mirror image of Consciousness, but only an image, which means it is not real. Mind is actually a twisted mirror, a circus mirror. Why? Well, in order for us to have the experience of ourselves as peace, love, joy, light and everything that we are; we had to create a world where there would be an imaginary absence of that. We needed the lack of love and peace so that we could have the experience of ourselves as that love and peace. That illusory lack of love is the opportunity for us to give and show the love that we are. If there were no lack, there would not be the opportunity for that certain fulfilling experience.

The best way for you to understand this is if you imagine that everything that exists is of white color. White universe, white stars, white planets, white sky, white rivers, white mountains, white things, animals and plants. Imagine that there is nothing else but white. Would it be possible to differentiate anything under such circumstances? Would we be able to have any experience? In fact, then we wouldn't have the words **color** or **white** because we wouldn't know that anything else exists. Everything we see would just be **That**. The word **white** can only exist when there is something that is not white. Only when a black or coloured spot would show up, we would get the experience of white because then there would be a contrast and a point of reference. In the moment you would see a black spot you would suddenly have the experience of whiteness that is all around.

In the same way, in order to have the experience of ourselves in all our highest qualities of love and peace, we had to create something that is opposite to that. And then we created the mind, which is, by its own character, pessimistic, negative, angry, restless and everything that we, as Consciousness, are not. We created it to be like that so that we could have all those experiences. Consciousness and mind are like white and black color. Don't expect your mind to be the Consciousness because you are the Consciousness and you don't need your mind to be such. Expect your mind, at least in the beginning, to be the opposite of yourself, to be a monkey mind, so it could give you a chance to show who you really are despite its challenges.

As Is the Thought, So Is the Life

Thoughts are the basis of this manifested universe, and the mind is actually the set of thoughts. All thoughts together form the mind. This whole manifested universe, everything you see; everything you can touch, smell, taste, hear, is the result of thought; is the result of the imagination of the mind; not just the individual mind, but the global and universal mind. Thoughts are the ones that give us the impression of everything we see. The thought is the first step in order for something to be created. The Universe was created as a thought. It is like that in your life too; everything in it is first created in the thought. Thoughts are the basis of everything that you live for and everything that you see.

Consciousness first has a thought and the imagined picture about something that it wants to experience. After the thought there comes the sound (saying of the thought). After the sound comes your feeling about that idea, then practical rational thoughts, then emotions in the body and at the end, the physical acting so that the idea could be realised.

- Practice for the Day -

Pay attention to the thoughts that fill your head every day. Keep in your mind only those thoughts which you want to experience in the physical world, which you want to see and feel as real. Consciously and intentionally fill your thinking only with the things you want to experience, even if in the beginning there is no visible result. Be persistent and consistent and you will turn the flow in other direction.

Awareness of Thoughts

When we are conscious of the thoughts, they are still there, but we don't identify with them anymore. We detach ourselves from our attachment to them, from identifying with them.

Then you can choose:
Do I like this thought? No.
Does it help me in life? No.
How do I feel because of it? Bad.
Do I like feeling bad? No.

In that case you can choose some other thought! There are a billion of them so you can just choose. On the other hand, when do thoughts become yours? It happens when you hold them, when you enter into them. It's the same as when you are waiting for a bus or a tram at a station, and bus number six which you don't need, arrives but you still get on it. Then you drive around the town for nothing. However, when you realise that you are on a bus that is not going where you want to go, you just need to get off and look for the one that is going where you want to be. The same is with the thoughts.

Most of the Thoughts Are Like City Buses

Most of the thoughts do not exist in your head. They exist in the mental field, which pervades the whole Universe, including collective mental fields where you live and work. Your body, like an antenna, catches these thoughts that already exist and that go through your energy field. Thoughts are like city buses that follow their schedule from a specific starting point to a specific predetermined destination. Each line of a city bus goes to exactly the determined place by the exactly determined route. The same is true with thoughts. Each of them has its own route and its own destination. Thoughts based on fear do not lead to love. Thoughts based on poverty and hardship do not lead to abundance. Thoughts about illness do not lead to health. **A thought leads to the content with which it is filled.**

- Practice for the Day -

Thoughts will go through your head like city buses, but nobody is forcing you to get on them. Stay at the station and observe consciously which thought has come and where it goes. Don't get inside those that do not lead to where you want to go. Wait and observe. If you don't use certain thoughts for a long time they will be eliminated, just like a bus line of the city transport which no one is using any more.

Types of Thoughts

In addition to the thoughts that are like buses and that already exist in the mental field and go through your mind on their own pre-established schedule and without your will, there are other types of thoughts which you can have in your mind.

There are taxi thoughts, which you can invoke. For example when you intentionally and consciously decide that you want to go to a certain place and you deliberately fill your mind with the thoughts that lead there. Those are affirmative and similar to positive thoughts and affirmations.

There are also creative thoughts that are like owning a car, a four-wheel-drive car. These are the thoughts that exist in the process of imagination. There are literally no limits with these thoughts; we can drive those thoughts in our mind wherever our heart desires. Everything is possible and we can go wherever we want. In time, this ability of imagining evolves so that such thoughts take us with high speed into the realisation, as if we have replaced the car by a rocket.

- Practice for the Day -

Spend some time every day in relaxation by feeling the desires and ideas of your heart and allowing yourself to imagine them. See yourself as if you were already living what you are dreaming about, in each and the smallest detail. Allow yourself to be guided by imagination and don't put limits that something might be impossible at any moment. While you are imagining, notice how you feel. The feeling is the key.

Don't Own the Thoughts

We are aware that our mind in under the influence of others and of our environment, that they are manipulated, and that the majority of thoughts are not ours. It is best if you do not own thoughts at all. When you hear yourself saying, "Here, this thought is torturing me, I cannot stop thinking", you should realise that it is not your thought. Please understand that. They are there, like a bus at your station, and the thought that you pay attention to will be caught. When you enter into it, it will lead to an emotion, like anger, anxiety, restlessness or whatever its destination is. When you notice that you are starting to catch a thought, just refocus yourself consciously. When a negative thought occurs, get out of it just as you would get off the wrong bus. You can intentionally replace it by a positive one; invite some other, positive thought, as you would call a taxi.

- Practice for the Day -

Right now when you are overwhelmed with thoughts that lead to painful or unwanted experiences, become aware that you are riding on the wrong bus in the direction where you don't want to go to. And right now, on purpose, say something opposite to what your thoughts are telling you. As much as it seems silly, hard or fake, think and say the thought that you wish to be fulfilled.

Positive and Negative Thoughts

A Master does not judge her or his thoughts; a Master does not say these are good, and these are bad. There isn't such thing as good or bad thoughts. Good thoughts could be those thoughts that take you where you want to go and bad thoughts could be those that take you away from where you want to go. When we say that some thought is good or bad, it can also be defined in relation to its positive or negative electric charge. Every thought has an electric charge, which can be scanned by some sophisticated devices, and this charge is measured in microwatts at negative potency. Although that electric charge is very small, every thought has it. Hence, thoughts are physical and can be strong or weak. Considering that, a Master chooses thoughts with a stronger electric charge and those that will bring him the things he intends to create in his or her life.

Even One Thought Based on Love Is Enough

As Dr, David R. Hawkins discovered and wrote in his book Power vs. Force, one thought based on love has 715 millions potencies higher electric strength in micro-watts, which is 10 on 715 million higher potency than a thought based on fear. That means that one thought based on love at the end of the day can annul a whole chain of thoughts based on fear, anger, indignation, guilt, jealousy or pride.

- Practice for the Day -

Start the day with at least one thought filled with gratitude, compassion, care, understanding and acceptance. During the day think of something that opens your heart and puts a smile on your face. End the day with at least one thought based on love and gratitude. Even one such thought can make a significant change. Many such thoughts could change everything. One by one.

I Choose to Have Only Positive Thoughts in My Mind

A person who knows who she/he is has awareness that every thought he/she focuses on will start to manifest itself in action and experience. Such a person has experienced things with both negative and positive power and will tell herself, "I prefer the positive. I have nothing against the other ones, but they don't suit me. Since I know that every thought leads to the material form of itself, I choose to have only positive thoughts in my mind. For when I have the negative ones, then they happen, and I don't need that; I don't like it. That is all. I don't judge them; I don't say that they are bad. They are not bad. I just don't prefer them. They cause me pain. And I don't like to suffer." Just be aware that you are the one who chooses, the one who can bring about change for you.

Stop Fighting Your Thoughts

You are not your thoughts; it is something you pay attention to. You are neither the source nor the cause of majority of your thoughts. So stop fighting with them and stop criticising yourself for the thoughts you have. You did not create them and you are not them. All those thoughts exist in the field around and without you. You don't have to be present in order for those thoughts to exist. Inside this manifestation, there are all kinds of thoughts – thoughts full of love and thoughts full of fear and full of murders, full of restlessness and anger, full of compassion and joy and happiness. There are all kinds of thoughts. What you should do, what is your only responsibility in that regard, is to choose which ones you will pick, what you will focus on.

- Practice for the Day -

When you notice that you are torturing or criticising yourself because of a thought that you have or say and do, stop immediately in that moment. Exhale and say to yourself, "These are not my thoughts. In this moment I am using my responsibility and my power to not participate in verbalising or acting upon such thoughts. I let them be. I am not fighting, and I am not giving them importance." Then you can return your attention to the center of your chest, to your heart energy center, and notice how you feel there. Keep your attention on the feeling in the heart.

Practice Makes the Master

Also in the state of high consciousness it can happen that a negative thought crawls into the mind. In the high consciousness it can happen that a negative thought slips in. If such a negative thought occurs, you can replace it with a positive one. You simply replace it, like an object that is defective. You intentionally focus on something else. You can notice and realise that negative thoughts have crawled into your mind, and that you have increased them and expanded them so that they became yours. In that moment you can intentionally and consciously focus on something else. You can refocus your attention on something else. That is a practice of spiritual awareness.

- Practice for the Day -

If you are overwhelmed by unwanted thoughts and you do not have the ability to replace them by opposite ones, then at least focus on something that is beautiful or good in your surroundings. Find something that you will be able to give a positive comment. Maybe it is clear skies, maybe a beautiful painting on the wall, maybe a flower or some color. Anything, just to move your focus from what you really do not want. That is always the first step. Inhale, exhale and relax for a few moments in the goodness or beauty of what you see.

The Energy Goes to What You Are Focusing on

A famous saying by Anthony Robbins says, "Where focus goes, energy flows." If you focus on negative thoughts that exist independently from you, they will occupy the space of your mind. When they enter the space of your mind, they do have the ability to get inside on their own without your invitation; it is up to you if you will keep them and make an elephant out of a little mouse. There lies your responsibility and your freedom of choice. That is where you are a creator. If you focus on something that you don't want, the energy goes to that which you do not want and makes it grow and become stronger. If you focus on something you want to experience, energy goes to that. Energy is completely indifferent to what you will focus on. Energy is like a Genie in the bottle that is waiting for your command and is not judging your choices.

- Practice for the Day -

Notice how during the day your focus goes to different things. Notice what is useful for you, and what is harmful. What is taking you to the future that you would like to experience, and what is taking you away from it? When you catch yourself focusing on unwanted things, take a deep breath and exhale saying, "I will not feed this since I do not want it to grow. I choose to feed the things that I want to grow." For the start, at least stop watching TV news and bloody criminal series and reading daily newspapers. They will fill your mind with the future you do not want to create and live.

True Responsibility

Thoughts are seeds that fall into your mind without your control, but what you do with them in your mind is your responsibility. The seed itself is not the problem. The problem is what happens when you pursue that thought, when you grow the initial thought, when you expand it and spin it for days inside yourself, when you cannot sleep, when you have dialogues in your head and when you plan in advance what you will say to somebody and what they will reply, then what you will say back to them and how you will have a good fight.

The same as you plan the whole fight in your head, the same as you remember all the things that others didn't do and that will annoy you when you see them, the same as you plan what you will say to them when you see them; in that same way you can plan that everything will be all right. But no, for some reason we choose the first fighting option as if we enjoy it, as if we like to have a fight, as if we are bored and missing the excitement. Why would we have something nice if we can have it the ugly way? Why would we imagine the positive outcome, when we can plan the worst-case scenario? And then, when that quarrel that you imagined and planned in your head happens, you say, "I knew it. I expected it to be just like that."

- Practice for the Day -

Other people are not the trash bins for our frustrations, although it seems that they are the cause of those frustrations. I am not suggesting that you ignore your anger and dissatisfaction with somebody or something. By no means! I am just encouraging you not to spend your energy needlessly planning and projecting a hard or painful future in advance. Only that is needless. Take a moment to remember a situation when you wasted your energy in such a way and what was the result. Is there a situation right now in your life that you could handle in a different way? Allow yourself to be neutral in advance and in the moment of talking. In this situation, feel what is coming to be said or done spontaneously. You have the right to say if something is making you angry or dissatisfied, but you don't need days to imagine the dialogues because then they will not be fresh in the given moment.

Freedom of Choice

"Life is like a game of cards. The hand you are dealt is determinism; the way you play it is free will."

- Jawaharlal Nehru

Look and Stop

What is it that does not serve you in life? What? Which attitudes, beliefs, opinions, demands, desires, expectations? What is not serving you anymore? Where do you spend your energy, your life breath: to serve a monster that has grown too big? Where are you killing yourself serving something that is not you? Stop it, today.

- Practice for the Day -

There is something that died a long time ago, that has dried up like an old branch of a tree and has no more use in your life; and you let yourself drag it along with you. Discover today the belief, expectation or opinion that is no longer based on your current experience because life has shown you long ago that it is not like that any more. The same way we have accepted one day that the Sun does not rotate around the Earth, you will have to accept that that belief is no longer true in your life. To start, you can stop telling yourself lies, and then in time you will stop living them.

Choose

In each life situation when you feel bad, you have a choice to go on feeling like that or to decide to change it in yourself. You have a choice and just need to decide.

- Practice for the Day -

The first step of every transformation is the decision that you don't want to live and feel like you had until then. Even if you don't know how to do it differently, at least decide that you will not do it like before and that something has to change. Then, relax physically and allow Life to bring you the thing that will make that transformation possible. Next, pay attention to what starts to show up in the form of information or adds on the Internet, in talks with your friends, on the radio or in songs. You will see that things you need to do or where you need to go are coming to you. The Life knows! Let it guide you.

Your Choice

When you realise that you can choose, then you can change your mind. As long as you don't know that you are the one choosing, you consider yourself a victim. And being in the state of victimhood is the biggest negation of your Divine nature.

- Practice for the Day -

What are the situations where you say you don't have a choice and that you simply have to be in it? As long as you have that opinion the things will look the same. You always have a choice, even if only between two terrible options which do not seem like you have a choice at all. In order to get out of that lie of not having a choice, start by saying the truth, "I know I have a choice, but in this moment I am choosing to be in this situation because for some reason it is easier than the other options. At the same time, I am opening myself to Life to show me the better options so that I could feel what to do next." When you say that, even if nothing changes, at least you are not the victim, but a free man that chooses and accepts life experiences. In that way you have started expressing your Divine nature.

Don't Fall Into the Trap

The thing that most often encourages negative thoughts is falling into the trap of the existence of the victim and the felon. When we see ourselves as a victim of somebody's actions then we can detect the negative thoughts about that person forming immediately. Observe the situations and temptations where you start criticising, attacking or blaming other people, circumstances or events. Observe if you are feeling like a victim of somebody's behaviour. Negative thoughts are just a signal that you are not in balance and that the mind and ego have overtaken the control over your life.

- Practice for the Day -

The feeling of victimhood is not necessary for you to do what you need to do in order to correct an injustice or get what belongs to you. A victim does not have the strength to act because it lost its power. The feeling of being a victim is an unnecessary factor on the path to justice. First you need to get angry, but not at others. Get angry at that state in which you are living. Get angry with yourself because you are allowing yourself to stay at the bottom of human consciousness. Get up and feel your dignity and pride, and then bravely say your truth. Say what you really need and feel. Say what you are looking for. Speak to Life and tell it, "I let you guide me to all the places, to all the people, to all the solutions and ideas so that I would get what you have prepared for me. I am ready."

You Are Not

You are not your thoughts, you are not your emotions, you are not your opinions, ideas, plans, likes or dislikes, and you are not your beliefs or attitudes. You are not any of that. None of that exists to be served by you. It only exists to serve you, when and if you need it to.

- Practice for the Day -

Do you spend hours, days or your lifetime serving an idea, a plan or a belief? Do you waste energy defending your attitudes and beliefs? Do you argue about perceptions of a job or the world? If you do, you are wasting your precious time on Earth. You are not a machine made to serve opinions or ideas. They are there to serve you. If they are not making your life easier, then you don't need them. Take a few moments now to become aware of and write down:

- *Any ideas, plans or beliefs that you serve and invest your time, money and energy in.*
- *Any attitudes or beliefs that you keep justifying or defending in front of others.*
- *Any arguments you keep having with others based on the difference of perceptions of a situation or the world at large.*

Then take a look at which of those you took to make your life easier or manageable and which of them are no longer serving that purpose, but are making your life more difficult and exhausting. You can then choose not to be their slave any more.

My Experience Is the Measure of My Evolution

We just need to be aware that an experience is a decision. We make those decisions every single moment of every single minute; always and forever. Every moment offers countless possibilities of experiencing ourselves the way we know ourselves. We can always choose to be love or fear, to be truth or lie, to be God or separated from God, to be violent or non-violent, and so on. Not just that we can choose, **we are already choosing**. To be a God, means to have the power to choose to experience Love because you ARE Love, to experience kindness because you ARE kindness, to choose peace because you ARE peace.

- Practice for the Day -

If you choose to Be peace, be that peace today while you are driving your car through a traffic jam.
If you choose to Be patience, be that patience while you are waiting in line in front of a counter.
If you choose to Be tolerance, be that tolerance at work.
If you choose to Be tenderness, be that tenderness today with yourself.
Whatever you choose, Be it today in at least one situation.
Just once today. And likewise every today.
That is your evolution!

I Choose to Be ...

Next time when you are faced with a situation or a choice, just stop for a moment and observe. Observe yourself. Observe your reactions. Observe your thoughts. And then choose to be who you really are. In the moment of the greatest fear, choose to be fearless, because you know that you are eternal pure Consciousness, pure Love. In the moment of the greatest sorrow choose to be joy because you are unmoved by the world drama. Just don't pretend and lie to yourself. Admit to yourself every feeling that comes. Allow yourself to be sad, angry, or whatever. God is everything so don't judge and don't refuse any part of your being. Just be aware that you are choosing to be that. And if you don't like it, choose differently. If you don't like to be angry, choose to be in peace. If you don't like to be sad, choose to be happy.

Your choice, your decision, is the first step in life bringing you the solution and guidance for the change of your state of being.

The Show of Your Life

"All the world's a stage, and all the men and women merely players; They have their exits and their entrances; And one man in his time plays many parts."
- William Shakespeare

World Is a Stage and You Are an Actor

The world and the whole Universe are a stage where the show of your life is happening. Souls are the actors in different roles and different physical forms, and at the same time they are co-creators of the script. The Highest Consciousness is the director of the film, and the mind is the cameraman and the projector of the film.

Places where you live and work are the stage of your life's theatre play, of your film. You, as a soul, are the actor that is behind your current role with your name both given and surname. That personality, the person you play, has its past, genetic heritage, character traits, typology of personality, parents and family, talents, flaws and virtues, sex, sexual and gender orientation, and beliefs. All the other people in your life are roles that are played by other close souls. The problem is that you have forgotten that you are playing those roles and now you believe you are them. The mask has glued itself to the face of the actor and the actor does not remember what he/she is like without that mask.

- Practice for the Day -

Take a look now at all the roles that you play and all the masks that you wear. What are the segments of your life where you have completely identified yourself with the role, forgetting your Divine nature?

Notice Your Influence

Notice how you are acting and apply it to everything in life. Notice how your state of consciousness influences all the people around you and changes their mood. Notice how your anxiousness influences others, but also how your joy influences them. Just be aware of your influence and the mutual influence.

Where Is the Script of Your Life Created?

You are aware that you're not your thoughts, that you didn't create them, that you are not their source and that you are not responsible for those thoughts. You are responsible for taking those thoughts, for building them up and for processing them. Instead of going around the world fixing what you see, trying to fix other people, some injustices, state laws, history, things that others did and shouldn't have done, correcting wars, riots, hunger and the economic crisis. You should discover another path. Instead of going around and solving things on the stage, it is important that you realise that things are really not done that way. Look at soap operas or theatre plays – actors on the stage act and follow the script. The act is created and changed in the room where the scriptwriters write, not on the stage or on the film set, but in the script-writing room. The script-writing room is in your mind and in your heart. It is in your imagination. That is where you can change the script because you, as a soul, are a co-scriptwriter.

- Practice for the Day -

Before you start doing something, first in your heart and in your imagination feel, imagine and design a script that you want to experience physically through the body and the five senses. See and feel inside yourself solutions that you want to see in the outside world and after that start doing. The script goes before acting.

Consciousness Changes the Flow of Life

In the show of your life you are not the only scriptwriter. The Highest Self (often known as God) is the main scriptwriter, and then there are sub-scriptwriters because it is a big show where not everything is written in advance. It is written along the way, in cooperation between the souls and the Highest Self. We are co-creators of this manifestation, and not individual nor independent. It is impossible to be an independent creator when you are surrounded by millions of other living beings on a living planet in a living solar system in a living galaxy in a living Universe. However, you have the influence and you have the ability to write parts of your script. As we have been discussing, you are capable of changing everyday things, your focus, and your state of consciousness. The moment when your state of consciousness changes, the scenography changes. Everything you see is the reflection of your consciousness, of your present state of consciousness: Absolutely everything. If your consciousness is in the mud, then you see mud around you. If your consciousness is high, then you are like a bird, you see things from a better perspective; you see the whole city and the sea and what is behind the mountains. In that way you get a completely new impression of the world. But all of that is based on your decision about what you will focus on.

You Are the Star and the Main Role in Your Life

All the people you see are the actors and they are playing in the play that you are writing in collaboration with God. You are the main role in your life, not somebody else. Others are main roles in their lives. When someone else is the main role in your life, the problem occurs, since everything is created so that everyone is the main role only in their own life. In the film of your life you are the main star, and the others are the supporting roles. Don't try to be the main role in somebody else's life or allow that somebody else be the main role in your life. The thing that happens when people make another person the icon of their life, and when everything is dedicated and subordinated to that person, is that they end up in dissatisfaction, misery and bitterness.

- Practice for the Day -

Think and feel to whom you have given the power over your life. Who did you put on the first place, and made yourself inferior to them? Take a moment to think who or what has become the meaning of your life? It is time to get your power back to yourself and put yourself on the first place where you naturally belong. You can do that by deciding to dedicate time to your needs and wants, to feel what would make you happy and then give it to yourself. Maybe you need rest and relaxation, or travel and time alone. Maybe you would like to explore your artistic side or start doing some sport or join a social club. On top of that, it is likely that you will need to pull away your servility of others that they got used to. If those that took the first place in your life are now able to take care of themselves, let them do it.

Once you have removed others from the pedestal of your life, you will need to become aware in whose life you have imposed yourself to be on the first place. It is time to let them get back their own power as well. Take time to notice whom you are trying to control, or call many times a day, or require them to ask you for advice or permission, or expect them to meet your needs. Does anyone feel suffocated by your presence? A good way to begin would be to honestly ask your dear ones whether they feel imposed by your requirements.

Don't Fight With Life

You don't have to fight against anything. What's the use of fighting? You can simply stop feeding the things you feel do not belong in your life any more. And that's their end. Some Native Americans believe you have two wolves inside yourself, one is good and one is evil. The one you feed will win. So, you don't have to fight against anything, you just stop giving it your energy.

- Practice for the Day -

Become aware now of the areas or situations in life where you are constantly fighting and where you feel exhausted. Your fighting feeds the enemy. Just give up the fighting because you cannot beat Life. Give up your fight against Life before you die. Inhale and exhale with relaxation and feel how you are waving a white flag of surrender. Tell yourself, "I surrender! I cannot fight any more. I have reached the bottom. Let it be as it should be. I surrender to Life!" Then you will see that hidden forces of Life will move, which will give you the strength and harmony with the flow of Life. Then your fight will become a constructive action in a certain direction.

Why Shame and Guilt?

Anyone can do something that they could regret, irrespective of the level of consciousness they live in. When you realise that you are doing something that is not right or is not good for you, in case that your ego is ruling you then you will fall into the states of shame and guilt and you will stay there for a long time, and those are two of the lowest states of consciousness. Ego will say, "How could I have done it; I am a terrible person; Will they be able to forgive me?" When ego is in charge of you, it wants you to be in the lowest possible state of consciousness, because the lower the consciousness the stronger the ego.

If, on the other hand, Consciousness is ruling your life, it will realise that something negative was done that should not have been done. It will feel shame and guilt for a while, for a few seconds or minutes, but then it will say, "This is not something to be done, but I did it. What can I do to make it right?; What can I do now?" There will be no more shame or guilt, as they are just messages that something should not be done. It is like when you burn yourself on a stove, and then you know that hot surfaces should not be touched. You will just ask yourself what you will do from then on, and then it will become clear. After that you go on. No more past, no resentment. You go on and you act on the basis of this awareness and decision.

- Practice for the Day -

Is there something that is keeping you in the state of shame and guilt? Come on, become aware of that situation, conclude what the lesson is and decide how you will behave from now on in similar situations when they come up. Say that you are sorry and express a true regret for the things done in the past, and after that don't look back. Your change of behaviour is the best apology. Just move forward. God put the eyes on the front part of your head because you need to look forward and walk forward. Stop turning backwards because it is dangerous considering you don't see where you're going then.

Up - Down

Your level of consciousness will go up and down. You should know, there will be beautiful days, but also there will be very ugly days. Sometimes everything will be very easy, and sometimes very difficult. But that is how it goes. It cannot go straight. A straight line on the heart rate monitor in the hospital means that you are dead. Nobody wants a flat line in the hospital; everybody wants the line to go up and down. It is the same with consciousness; it goes up and then down. Life and energy also go up and down. Success, health, love, joy, pleasure and everything else that we want to keep in continuity increases and decreases too. It is fine that everything happens like that and you don't have to apologise to anybody about it. You don't have to blame yourself when you are down nor praise yourself when you are up.

Now and Here

When Consciousness is ruling your life, then there is neither past nor future because Consciousness is only now and here. Where are the problems and concerns; where is the job and people that you have a problem with? When Consciousness dwells somewhere, it is present; there is no other place and time: just now and here. And when Consciousness is present, it is clear to you what you need to do in that moment: not tomorrow, but now; the answer is always in the present moment.

- Practice for the Day -

Notice if you are focused on what is now in front of you or on something that happened or might happen? Turn around yourself and look inside of you to notice what is here now. Just be now with the pictures, sounds, sensations and emotions that are present in the moment, without analysis and condemnation, without thinking about the consequences in the future. Just be here with what is present now. Your conscious presence is the biggest gift.

In the Present Moment

Mind will always go one step further into the future and think: And what if? You can then say, "I am here now, no 'what if' and when. When something happens, then I will know. In the present moment I always know what I should do. In the present moment I am the omnipotence and omniscience."

The Power of Gratitude and Love

"I think that modern medicine has become like a prophet offering a life free of pain. It is nonsense. The only thing I know that truly heals people is unconditional love."
- Elisabeth Kübler-Ross

Gratitude

Sometimes it is good to be in a situation where there is no comfort that we are used to because then you see that you can live without a lot of things. That is liberation. We think that we are free people, but most of us are enslaved. We are so conditioned by different things, places, people, habits and jobs that there is simply no freedom. When you start observing your life, you see that you are not free, and you thought you were. You are not independent, you thought you were. A complete independence cannot exist as long as you have a body. And that is where the gratitude comes from. When you realise how much your life depends on a million different things that exist not just on this planet, but also in the wider universe; that is when you can feel gratitude. Until then it is just a mental process, and mental gratitude is a broken version of the true gratitude of the heart.

- Practice for the Day -

Right now look around you and feel gratitude for at least one thing or person and everything that contributes to your life.

All of Creation Supports Your Life

Realise how the whole world, all of creation, supports your life and how every breath you take depends on everything around you. Your every day depends on hundreds of strangers. Every day you go shopping and you grab something from the shelf not wondering where it came from. The fact that you pay for it does not mean that you realise what is behind it. You probably don't ask yourself who is behind every product on the shelf, how many hundreds of people, how much work on the land and of the farmers, how many people on the rigs that take the oil out so that the trucks could come to your supermarket, how many people are working so that you can just walk into a supermarket and take what you want. If you knew how much effort and work and organisation of the whole planet is involved in making your life easy, how grateful you would be walking around. That is gratitude, when you realise the greatness of the system that supports your life.

- Practice for the Day -

Feel gratitude because you have running tap water in your home, and you don't have to go to some well carrying buckets of water on your head. (If you do have to walk to a well carrying buckets of water on your head, probably you already feel gratitude for the fact that there is a well and that there is water in it). Feel gratitude because you can walk into a supermarket and just choose what you will eat from the shelf, without having to grow it for months and worry if it will succeed. Feel gratitude for everything that you have been taking for granted until now.

Discover Paradise

Be truly grateful, not just for something that is, but also for something that isn't. Be grateful in advance, and it will happen. Even if it still hasn't happened, you can be grateful as if it has already happened, and then it will happen. That feeling of true gratitude from the heart is the thing we need to live with every day. When you are truly grateful in your heart, then you are in Paradise, in that beautiful place. Actually, it is already beautiful and it just needs to be discovered. It needs to be cleaned, the dirt needs to be removed and then you will see the gold under it. Gold is in our hearts and all we need to do is remove the dust and cobwebs of the thoughts and injuries that hide it.

The Power That Moves the Universe

True gratitude is the power that moves the Universe. It is the power with which a master lives his life, with which he creates. It is the power that made Jesus walk on water, bring the dead back to life, create fish in the net and turn water into wine. That power means going with full trust and complete feeling of gratitude that all is possible, beyond any doubt and without suspicion. When you do it with such a feeling, like Jesus, then it has to happen. The whole Universe is a manifestation of such a feeling. When the Universe notices true and unconditional gratitude for something in your heart, then it makes sure that it becomes real because you cannot be grateful for something that does not exist. Your true gratitude is the command to the Universe for something to be, in case it already isn't.

The Almighty Love

Love is indeed almighty and everything that is based on unconditional and unreserved love has the ability to annul anything based on fear. But the choice is yours again. You have to choose.

- Practice for the Day -

Find the strength and say, "Do I need this, where is this taking me?" Decide not to act on the basis of the world that is not real, on the basis of emotions that are made up and the thoughts that are not yours. Decide to act on the basis of love.

I Love Myself Completely, Just as I Am

In order to start loving ourselves completely, we need to be sure that we don't have anything against ourselves. Get rid of condemning yourself because you are perfect the way you are. If you don't like some part of your being, just decide not to behave like that anymore. But first let go of resentment towards yourself. Forgive yourself, forgive, forgive. If you find some negative aspects of your current personality, just throw them away as a piece of old clothing. It has served its purpose and it is no longer needed. You didn't know better before, but now you do.

- Practice for the Day -

Take some alone time and contemplate about if there is something in your past or present part of life that you are holding against yourself, that you resent in yourself. If there is, forgive yourself everything. Accept that.

The Basis of Living Without Resentment

FORGIVING IS SOMETHING THAT IS DONE AND FELT. It happens with a conscious decision that we will let go of resentment and will forgive. In the highest consciousness we forgive everything to everybody, including ourselves too, because in the high consciousness **we know that there is nothing to forgive**. This realisation and the true acceptance of the fact that there is nothing to forgive, if we get into that state of mind completely, brings us all-pervading transformation of every aspect of your life.

- Practice for the day -

Become aware if you are feeling resentful of yourself about something, or to somebody or something. Is there something that you didn't let go of or you didn't say? Resenting and being angry with somebody is like drinking a poison expecting it to kill them. In fact, that poison is poisoning us so it needs to be allowed to leave and be healed*.

* It is not possible to describe the process of letting go of resentment and forgiveness in short in this book; it should be lived through with the guidance of the therapist or a healer. On our YouTube channel there is a whole recorded seminar on forgiveness and the guided healing process for letting go of resentment under the Playlist called Forgiving.

Practical Expressions of Love

Love is practical, not abstract and conceptual. Love is work; Love is something that we do; Love is action. In our behaviour it is expressed as respect, understanding, acceptance, care, compassion and freedom.

Love needs to exist in ourselves first so that it can be given to others. If you don't have a chocolate in your hand, then you cannot offer it around. First accept and give love to yourself, and then to everyone else. As the airplane crew tell us if we lose cabin pressure, you should first put the oxygen mask on your face, and then help others. That is because if you don't put the mask on yourself first, you can faint and then you cannot save others who need help and you have created a big problem for everyone who has to save you. People that don't love themselves become sick and then others have to love them and take care of them. Not loving ourselves is very selfish because it puts an unnecessary burden on others for something that we could have done ourselves.

- Practice for the day -

Become aware of how much you love yourself practically and how much you show it to yourself every day. Choose at least one deed that you will do today to demonstrate and give love to yourself.

Love As Respect

Loving yourself above all means respecting yourself. Respecting your time, space, knowledge, skills, work and effort. Appreciating who you are. Respect yourself, your time, your space, and your knowledge, and others will respect you and your needs too.

- Practice for the Day -

Right now, today, respect your time and don't wait for anybody who is late.
Today, leave work on time and don't stay longer than your working hours require.
Today, ask that in your space be as you want it, and not as others want.
Today, think how really big is the value of your work, on the basis of experience, knowledge, effort, time and expertise that you bring. Dare to communicate that to the outside world and feel that you have the right for a fair financial and material compensation and recognition.

After you have practiced respecting yourself, become aware how you are showing respect for others with your words and actions.

Love as Understanding

Understanding yourself means understanding your behaviour, your decisions, your emotions and your thoughts, and what has caused them. Everything that is happening now is the consequence of your previous decisions. If you don't like something about yourself, look where it is coming from and you will understand why you behave like that. You will see which person or event imposed such thinking or behaviour on your life. Understanding leads to acceptance, and in this way to forgiving yourself.

- Practice for the Day -

Right now, today, think about something that you don't like about yourself and take a look at the past, to what could have led to such a behaviour or habit. What were those circumstances and events that have conditioned you to such a life? Let understanding get into your awareness, and the compassion and tenderness will come with it. Compassion is the healing power of love.

When you become capable of understanding yourself, you can then start understanding your partner, children, parents, friends, colleagues and everything else. Let your compassion based on understanding heal the world.

Love as Acceptance

Acceptance is the first step of healing. When you understand and accept yourself just the way you are, then you will be able to forgive yourself. Actually, you will see that there is nothing to forgive because you didn't do anything wrong. As long as you deny some parts of yourself, they will continue to exist and will become louder because God does not cast off anybody or anything. Acceptance is pushing you to act in accordance with God and not cast away any part of yourself. When you accept a certain thing as an integral part of yourself, that is an expression of love, and love heals. We cannot change anything until we take it in our hands, until we accept it and grab it. Accepting gives you the power to do something with it.

- Practice for the Day -

Sit and relax, close your eyes, inhale and exhale with relaxation and feel what is that certain something you don't accept about yourself (a flaw, a character trait, a habit, a physical attribute and so on). Feel it in your chest. Then with both palms take it from your chest and hold it in front of you as if you are holding a bowl in your palms. Feel the weight of what you're holding in your hands. Feel its color, its texture and mass. Notice how it feels to hold that character trace or emotion. Then say in yourself, "I see this, but that is not really me. That is just a characteristic or a thing." Take a deep breath and exhale golden light into your palms. Exhale the heaviness from the chest. With exhaling and with the golden light and movements of your fingers and palms (as if you were kneading the clay) transform that characteristic into its opposite. Laziness can become proactivity, lying into honesty, fear into courage, and being late into punctuality. Notice how the weight in your hands is changing when the previous characteristic turns into the new one. Then press that new quality into your chest and squeeze your palms into the chest. Feel how the new quality is spreading through your chest, and then into the stomach and arms, and after that into the legs and neck and the head. Your whole body is permeated with this new quality. Hug yourself with your hands around your chest and shoulders. Stay hugged like that in acceptance of yourself.

Love as Care

Care is demonstrated as care for the body, mind and spirit. Pay attention to how you take care of your body. Everything that you put into your body and all the activities that you do have a low or high level of consciousness. After that pay attention to the things you feed into your mind, like what you read, watch, listen to and speak of. Thoughts are the language of the mind; emotions are chemical reactions of the body to the thoughts; feelings are the language of the heart; and actions are the language of the body.

Everything with which you feed your body and mind has a direct influence on emotions that appear. When you are emotionally not balanced, then your decisions and reactions will be mindless, hasty, conditioned and finally unwanted.

Pay attention to how you feed your spirit through meditation, sitting in silence, enjoying the beauty of life, dancing, singing, painting, bathing, swimming, walking through woods and so on. In reality you only have yourself, so be tender and don't lose the sole treasure that you can call your own.

- Practice for the Day -

Right this day show care towards every aspect of your existence.
Put into your body healthy food and water and breathe consciously for a few minutes. Spend at least half an hour exercising in some way.
Feed your mind with some nice and noble picture, a film, a text or a book and say something pleasant and positive.
Sing for the soul, dance, laugh or paint.
At the end look at how all of that has affected your emotional, psychological and physical state of being.
There is always one person that can show you care, and that is You.

Love as Compassion

Compassion is when we experience the state and feeling of others in their own skin and their own heart. Prejudices and condemnation disappear in compassion. Our thinking and mental control stop there while the heart takes the lead and connects us with the other being in order to understand and feel completely how the other feels. The power of compassion can then run through our heart with such force that it can produce an instant healing process or it might take us to a highly active physical level where we can help and where our own actions can eliminate the suffering. A spontaneous act of kindness and help can touch the hearts of millions of people and start an unstoppable transformation. Look at the people and the world with the eyes of compassion. Look at them with the eyes of love because when the light falls on the darkness, it disappears. The world needs your blessings and your look of love, not the look of contempt and disapproval.

- Practice for the Day -

When you find yourself criticising or blaming yourself or others, right in that moment do a process of understanding and let compassion expand itself. To receive understanding you can just say to yourself, "What has happened in the past that this person is behaving in this way?; They must have went through some painful experience to be living like this." Look at others in the eyes and feel how they feel. Your softness could be the cure for some of their old wounds.

Love as Freedom

Love is freedom because soul is freedom, and soul is love. Being Free means allowing yourself the freedom to be who you are, regardless of other people and situations. It means giving yourself freedom of expression of all other expressions of love: respect, understanding, acceptance, care and compassion. It means giving freedom to emotions, needs, fantasies, dreams, joys, fulfillments, and pleasures. If you don't allow that freedom to yourself, you will die while you are still in your living body. Then you will continue walking around like a zombi. It is not pleasant at all, and most of all unnecessary.

You are the judge, the jury, the accuser, the accused, the defence and the witness in the trial that you are running against yourself. You are the prisoner, the warden, the executioner and the prison guard in the prison of your life. You should know that the power of liberation and annulling the verdict lies only on you. The decision of the reduction of sentence is yours to make. The decision of releasing you from the prison is yours to make. If you don't want to free yourself, at least be gentle with yourself, with the prisoner, when you are playing the role of the prison guard.

- Practice for the Day -

Become aware of the parts of your life where you feel trapped, restricted or dead. What seems to be preventing you to be free in that area? Whom or what do you blame for your captivity? Can you, at the start, honestly and openly express how you feel? Can you admit what your needs and wishes are? Come on, it is just a small step of courage. The world will not collapse. You are more powerful and stronger than you think.

What Should I Do?

Sometimes we find ourselves wondering what to do next or how to resolve a situation. Our tendency is to usually go into our head and start thinking. In that way we ignore the real source of solutions.

- Practice for the Day -

Now pay attention to the center of your chest, where your energetic spiritual heart is, the point from where you spring into this world. Feel yourself completely there, now and here, In the heart. Inhale, close your eyes and while you are exhaling focus more deeply on the center of the chest. Stay focused there feeling and observing what is happening in the heart. Then imagine that you are making a decision A. Observe how does it feel in your heart while you see yourself in that decision. After that imagine that you are making a decision B. Observe how does it feel then. In which case is there heaviness, and in which lightness? Have you felt joy and a smile in your heart in one of the options? The option where you felt light is the truth, your true path.

Accept!

What is bothering you in this moment in your life, what don't you like, where does your ego have its liking or disliking, its opinion, its attitude or its belief? What would ego do if it was different, whom would it change, what does it expect from the others? Come on, remember, consciously and intentionally accept things just the way they are, right now. Stop being a servant to your shadow, because ego is nothing but a shadow. It is the shadow that you make on the ground while walking under the Sun. Stop serving your shadow! Simply accept what you were refusing to accept, accept it now. Order your shadow to accept. You accept it! Accepting is one of the practical expressions of love and the first step of the transformation of something.

As one day we have accepted that the Sun does not go around the Earth, in the same way we can accept everything else. We can simply accept a new truth, a new postulate, a new concept. There is no complicated process or procedure. We just accept that the things are not what we used to think they were. Your ego that comprehends the world through five senses cannot see the truth because its perception is relative and from limiting points of views. By only using our senses there is no way we could realise that Earth goes around the Sun. For our senses and our ego, the Earth is still and there is no proof that it is turning. Our eyes see that the Sun goes over the sky every day, so the only conclusion we could make based on the senses and limited thinking is that the Sun goes around the Earth. You cannot believe your senses and your limited ego experience.

- Practice for the Day -

Admit to yourself that through your five senses and through your mind you don't see the truth or the complete truth. Accept that things are not what you have thought they were. Accept that there is the bigger picture and open up to see and explore it.

Allow

"You have to take risks. We will only understand the miracle of life fully when we allow the unexpected to happen."
- Paulo Coelho

Allow and Let Go

Let go of all your plans, ideas, conceptions and opinions. Hand them over to life, hand them over to the *Source of Consciousness*. Give them to the river, like on a little boat, and let them leave. Let Life take them where they should go. Let go of control over every little thing and situation, just let it go. You don't need to worry where they will go. Trust that the intelligence of the Universe knows what is the best. This intelligence is pure love and joy. This intelligence is goodness and truth; it only wants the best for you. Let go. Let go of everything. Trust and experience the best.

- Practice for the Day -

Notice which ideas and plans create stress and tension for you. Where have you put deadlines and ambitions for yourself that only exhaust you while you try to realise them. Stress, tension, resistance and exhaustion are the proof that you are forcing something that is not a must. Cancel unnecessary stressful activities right now. Admit to yourself now that you don't have to. Feel that Life knows where you need to go and what you need to do. Take a deep breath, exhale with relaxation and tell yourself, "I will let the intelligence of Life guide me and lead this project. I am letting go of control over all that I don't control anyway. I am opening myself to receive what is best for me and what is the main thing for me to do." Keep on breathing, relaxing and feeling what it is like when you let go of control to the One who is more capable and intelligent than you.

Allow the Intelligence of Life

Allowing means that in spite of something you have conceived, you allow the possibility for it to be different than you have planned. You allow and are relaxed. You allow it to be the way you maybe haven't planned. You allow the intelligence of Life to act, to guide you, to take you and to bring you whatever you need. That intelligence which created everything, which conducts the whole creation, which takes care of the galaxies, suns, planets, seas, rivers and rains, takes care of you too. It is ready to do everything for you, and all you need to do is to allow it to do it. Without your permission it will not interfere in your life because it would be negating the freedom of choice that you were given at your birth. Freedom of choice is the greatest gift that we get at the beginning of our life. If you wish to do everything by yourself, by your own effort and struggle, by your own capabilities and ways, it will let you do it your way no matter how much you suffer and fail. Its hands are tied as long as you choose to do everything on your own.

However, should you choose to allow - in that same moment the whole power of the Universe would come to help you, to lift you and to carry you. Your allowing opens the doors to heaven and brings the help of the Source of Creation. You don't need to beg, ask, require or offer to trade. Just let it come into your life to do what is best for you. And when it does, don't tell it how and what to do. As soon as you know how something needs to be done, it gets out of your way and lets you do it yourself. Don't be like a child whose toy has broken and asks his/her father to fix it, only to tell him how to do it. Let the father do it as he knows, or do it yourself.

- Practice for the Day -

Inhale, exhale and tell yourself, "I allow the endless Intelligence of the Universe to guide me. I allow the Ocean of Life to carry me and to bring me everything I need. I allow Life to bring to me all the people and relationships, all ideas and solutions, all the opportunities and jobs, all situations and experiences and everything else that I need so that I can live my mission on Earth. I allow Life to take me to everything that I need. I completely, consciously and intentionally allow the higher Consciousness to guide me."

Bing Carefree Is the Key

In order for us to receive the guidance and help of the *High Consciousness*, so that the *Source of Creation* could completely take care of all our needs, there is only one condition. It is actually not a condition, but a way to unlock or lock the door, a way we open or close the tap for water. Water is always inside the pipes, but we need to open the tap so the water could run. It is pointless to stand in front of the tap and pray to God to send you water. Water is already there! Just let it flow. In the same way, help, support, guidance, and care of the *Source of Creation* is already here in our lives, all we need to do is let it flow and act.

The key for opening that door, the way to open that tap, is called **being carefree.** High Consciousness does not condition us by anything, but one of the laws of the Universe requires us to use our freedom of choice and to choose to receive the help. When we have a problem, then we have two simple choices: solving it on our own or allowing the Source to send the solution. The Source does not listen to what you say; it watches what you do and how you feel. You can be saying for days that you are allowing it to help you, but if your feelings and behaviour speak differently then it will listen to your behaviour. The only thing the Source watches in order to determine who is responsible for solving a problem is whether you **worry or not**.

If you are worried you are sending the message that responsibility is yours and that you are the one who needs to find a solution and resolve it. **If you are carefree**, then you are sending the message that the Source and the Universe need to find the solution that will, at the end, be carried out through your body and action. When you are worried, the ego has the control over your life. What your ego is actually saying is, "I believe that there is a God or a higher force, but this problem is so big that I will have to solve by myself." Your worry is a sign of the choice you made, and in that way you have closed the tap so that help cannot come to you. When you are carefree and worry-free, then you are showing through your behaviour and feelings that you trust the omnipotent and omniscient intelligence of the Source completely to solve even the biggest of problems. You trust its Love for you! Your carefree attitude is a sign of your transfer of control and responsibility to the One who really knows how to help.

- Practice for the Day -

If you have a problem, it is time to admit that you don't know how to solve it. Realise that worrying does not solve problems. Actions solve problems. Thinking that worrying will solve a problem is like expecting an egg to be boiled by looking at it. Eggs are not boiled by watching them, but by putting them in boiling water. Problems are not solved by worrying, but by inspiration, consideration and action or non-action. Take a deep breath, exhale with relaxation and say to yourself, "Worry does not solve problems. I choose to be carefree and to allow the Source to show me the solution and what I need to do." Then just look, feel, sit in silence, observe your breath and be open to receive the guidance for the thing you need to do. The solution will happen through your hands or the hands of other people.

Allow Everything That Is Within You

As you are allowed to live on Earth, you should allow everything that is within you to live in you. In spite of your reckless behaviour, polluting the environment, and spreading negative thoughts and emotions, planet Earth still allows you to live on its surface. When you discover emotions, thoughts, pains or discomfort within yourself that you would rather not have in your life, then it is time to allow them to be there. Your allowing will lead to healing. Allowing is a way for something uncomfortable within you to feel comfortable and loved and through that loving feeling to initiate the healing. Every illness is eventually just an indicator of the lack of love towards ourselves in some segment.

- Practice for the Day -

Lie down relaxed and focus consciously on the part of the body where there is a disease, pain, discomfort or emotion that bothers you. Go into that pain. Breathe into the pain or emotion and breathe out of it. You can speak to it, "Hi. I can see you and I allow you to be. I am sorry for ignoring you for so long. Now I am aware of your presence. I allow you to move as well. What is it that you would like to tell me?" Continuously observe what is happening in your body and consciously keep exhaling through your mouth and relaxing your muscles. Keep observing if the pain or emotion has a message for you, in the form of a thought or an image. Don't desire the pain to leave, just allow it be there the same way you are allowed to be on Earth. Let it move and express itself through a sound, voice, body movement, tears or laughter.

Allow All of the World

The first form of allowing was the one towards the Intelligence of the Universe. The second form was allowing everything within you. Allowing everything in the outside world is the third form of allowing. On the surface, this form of allowing looks like it has to do with other people and situations. It looks like we are allowing something from others, when actually it is only an inner process in which we bring ourselves into peace and relaxation about everything that is happening outside of us. When you allow within you that somebody does something outside then it cannot bother you because they are doing it with your permission, even without them knowing that you allowed it in the first place. Allowing is a way to stop the control of ego over your life. Ego will always object and get angry because of behaviour of other people, and allowing eliminates that anger because then other people do everything with your inner allowing. Allowing others to be what they are does not mean that you will physically support their behaviour or put up with the pain they are causing you. You will only allow them to be who they are, but you will not let them hurt you. Allowing is just an inner process to quiet your ego. I do not imply that you should verbally communicate to others that you allow their behaviour, which would likely be misunderstood.

- Practice for the Day -

When somebody in front of you is doing something that irritates you or if the driver of a car in the traffic annoys you, inhale and exhale focusing on the center of your chest and say to that man in yourself, "I allow you to do that, to act like that, to drive like that, to say that. Who am I to forbid you? Keep on. You can do it even more as far as I'm concerned. Come on, let me see for how long you can continue. I allow you." Notice how your inner tension is melting and disappearing with every exhale. Maybe you will start to laugh while you are saying those sentences. And then ask within yourself, "God, what happened to this person in their life when they are behaving so awfully? What kind of pain or trauma have they experienced? It must be very hard for them to live with that." Let the energy of your compassion spread through the space and start influencing everything.

Relaxing, Allowing, Surrendering

Relaxing is a physical activity, allowing is a mental activity, surrendering is a spiritual activity. The body relaxes, ego and mind allow, and the soul surrenders. Those are three levels of allowing: physical, mental and spiritual. Body is relaxed, mind allows, and soul surrenders. Each of them influences the other two and takes them with itself.

Surrendering

You surrender in the knowing that everything that should happen will come to you. Life will always give you more than you can imagine. You accept everything that is now here. There are no expectations, because expectations will lead you away from that state of harmony with Life and leave you in eternal anticipation, in a state where you are waiting for something to happen.

When you surrender you don't care what is waiting around the corner, you know that it will be fine. That is the difference, a big difference. You will feel it and notice it in yourself.

- Practice for the Day -

Lie down and relax. Feel how you are floating on the surface of the river of Life. It is carrying you and bringing you everything you need. You are lying on the surface of that mighty river which knows its destination and flows there carefree and relaxed. The river knows where it is going; it does not need your instructions. Just surrender to it. Breathe, enjoy and observe where it is taking you. Feel what is it like to be guided and carefree knowing that you are in the right hands.

Throw Yourself Into Life

Become aware now of the places where you control your life, what are the areas that your mind and your ego are controlling? What are they scared of; what are the things they won't let go; and what are the things they don't want to accept? What is that thing that is coming to your life and is scaring you so much that you are refusing, or that you cannot bear anymore? What are some other wishes of your mind, or some other urges, some other notions, or some other likings than what is present in your life at the moment? Become aware of them, accept that they are there and let them go. Allow them to be. Throw yourself into life. Throw yourself into the natural flow. Go into the situations or circumstances that are coming your way, into that something that seems to be scaring you. See your resistance and let it go because that is where you need to go. Don't follow the fear or wishes of your mind. Get into that which is in front of you now, into that which Life has brought and created for you. Dive into that. Life knows.

Reality

"Our intention creates our reality."
- Dr. Wayne W. Dyer

Pure Consciousness

When we dwell in the pure Consciousness, then we do not visualise, we don't think, we don't imagine, we don't project, we don't fall into any deliberate states of bliss, peace, serenity or love, and we don't do anything in order to get into a preconceived state because all of that would be yet another projection, artificially created from our mind. In the pure Awareness we don't have the intention to be in any particular state of being because that would again be a concept, a projection. Don't think that *Consciousness* is some blissful state, how would you imagine it if you have never felt it? Therefore don't imagine and don't project. If you have never felt peace, how would you imagine it now - by getting yourself into a states of illusion? Don't do it. Just be conscious, present and here with whatever is within you and around you. You are here, you are noticing. There is no sentiment, no romantic notion and you are not projecting anything. You just ARE, without an intention and desire that something should be a certain way.

- Practice for the Day -

Now become aware of the situation that you are in, of the space and people that surround you and of emotions and thoughts that are circulating through your body and mind. Become aware of the place from which you are aware of all of that. Where are you observing it from and who are you that is observing it all? Focus your attention on yourself as an observer and notice that those situations, the space, the people, thoughts and emotions are actually just objects of your awareness. You are the subject, and those are the objects. Keep attention on yourself as the one who is aware of all of that and therefore detached from it all.

In the Virtual Reality

If you don't succeed in getting into the state of the present moment, into the state of non-attachment to emotions, thoughts, the body and events around you, you will not liberate yourself from the virtual reality that we call our world. Every time you react based on the memories or old emotions, whenever you react from the past and on the basis of circumstances, people, society, fear, worry, thoughts, thinking or attitudes; you are attaching yourself more and more for the world of virtual reality, to the illusion that nullifies you as a being. In those moments you get weaker and are postponing the moment of awakening.

User In the Background

I like to say that the human physical appearance is like a bio-computer or a mobile phone. Just as a mobile phone has the body (hardware) so does a human being have a body made of bones, muscles and organs. Mobile phones have a screen and a camera, and humans have eyes. Mobile phones have a loudspeaker and a microphone, and humans have mouth and ears. Mobile phones have a battery, and humans have heart and blood. Mobile phones have a processor, and humans have their brains. Mobile phones have an operating system (software), and humans have mind and thoughts. Mobile phones are charged by electricity and humans by food, water and cosmic energy. Mobile phones can communicate with other mobile phones through GSM and WIFI networks, while humans do it through speech and writing. Mobile phones, like human beings, have something else in common and that is the fact that they are useless if there isn't the most important factor. That most important factor is the **User**, the one who is behind that device. The users of mobile phones are people, and who is the user behind human beings? That user we call the Spirit, Consciousness, Atma or Soul. That is the real You. You are not a human being; you are *Consciousness* that is behind and using its human form so it could have experiences and communicate with others through their own human forms. In order to exist, live and have experiences in this world we need bodies because otherwise we could not project and perceive this earthly appearance.

- Practice for the Day -

Today is a good day to start living more consciously aware that you are the One who is behind the eyes, behind the heart. You can start remembering yourself and your true reality by simple self-inquiry. Sit in a comfortable position, close your eyes and exhale with relaxation. You can then start asking yourself the following questions of you can have someone read them for you very slowly. After each question just observe the answer that appears by itself and then withdraw your attention to what remains when the senses and the mind disappear from the focus.

1. *If I would no longer have the eyes to see, would I still exists? Would something continue existing by itself?*
2. *If I would no longer have the nose or the thong to smell or taste the world, would I still exists?*
3. *If I would no longer have the sense of touch to feel the body and the outer world, would something here continue existing?*
4. *If I would no longer have the ears to hear, would I still exists?*
5. *Without the senses to perceive it how would I know that there is a world? Would there be a world for me?*
6. *Who am I that continues to exists even without the world?*
7. *If I would now forget all the past and memories, my name and origin, would it be possible for me to exist?*
8. *If I would drop all the plans for the future, could I still exist?*

Then simply let your attention rest in that which remains when everything else has fallen off.

What Is a Lie?

Everything in this world is a lie, just like your reflection in the mirror is a lie as well. Your belief that this world is real: that is that lie. This world is your imagination, a projection of the mind. It is a reflection of you as the spirit; it is just a mirror image of the one true reality, but not the reality itself. Do you renounce your belief in the reality of this world?

Reality

Unconditional, unrestricted Love is the only true expression of reality; it is the only thing that we can say really exists as a substance. Everything else is just a projection, a film screening, a game of light, a game of photons, an illusion.

Appearance

This visible world is not real. It is an appearance. An appearance is a visualisation, a 3D movie projection. It is a thing that appears and is not real. This world as an appearance comes from a projector, and that projector is in our hearts. Consciousness projects itself so it can see itself, so it can comprehend itself. Quantum physicists know that this world consists of atoms and that atoms are not fixed, that they don't have borders, but that they are events in time and space. Everything that atoms create is not real, but it appears as an event in time and space. If it can be seen, it is not real. If it can be heard, it is not real. If it can be tasted, it is not real. If it can be touched, it is not real. If it can be smelled, it is not real. If it can be changed, it is not real. If it has a beginning, it is not real. If it has an end, whenever it happens, it is not real.

Get to Know Yourself

If nothing is real, how will I see the Self then? How will I experience the Self, if it can't be seen and if it can't be touched? The Self can only be known and recognised.

What does it mean to recognise?
Recognise.
Re-cognise means that you already know it and you are getting to know it again.
Recognising means remembering that you know.
You will remember yourself; you will remember that you know yourself. You will come out of the oblivion.

Silence

Silence is the food for the main aspect of yourself, for your true self. Silence provides the opportunity for withdrawing the attention from the senses and the mind to the eternal existence that you really are.

- Practice for the Day -

Go into silence every day, both verbally and mentally.
Just be quiet.

Awakening

Your own awakening will free you from the teacher and the teaching. It will have to liberate you. First you will apply these messages and teaching, and then one day you will drop it just like children give away old clothes as they grow up. And you will have to drop it all because otherwise it could turn into a dogma or a religion. You will know when the moment of awakening comes.

Ivan Bava: Answers from Within

About the Author

Ivan Bava is an awakened master of non-duality, allowing and surrender to the Flow of Life. A disciple of Sathya Sai Baba, he was born in Croatia as Ivan Bavcevic and graduated from the Rochester Institute of Technology to later become an international lecturer, therapist and life sciences teacher with his **School of Awareness and Spiritual Mastery** established in Spain, Slovenia, Croatia and occasionally in and other countries. Bava holds his programs directly in Spanish, English and Croatian, giving people the opportunity to have access to the most important life knowledge in their mother tongue. He is also a visiting lecturer at the University of Granada, the most prestigious Spanish university that is 500 years old and has 80,000 students per year. Every month he teaches hundreds of students and the public audiences practical disciplines for conscious and advanced life as a master over your own mind, emotions and body. He is a frequent guest in various radio and TV shows.

From 2012 till 2023 he has travelled more than 700.000 kilometres and gave more than eight thousand hours of lectures, workshops and healing sessions. In his work with tens of thousands of people, Ivan has seen that there is a huge inner struggle and lack of acceptance of oneself in the majority of the population. There is continuous effort for self-improvement, self-correction, inner criticism, self blame and quilt. There seems to be, what Bava calls, an *Inner Terrorist* that tortures us psychologically and emotionally. All of this separates us from the Peace that is part of our very being and puts us purely in a mind that never rests. Bava uses his **ALO Method** (Allow, Let Go, Surrender) to give people possibility for liberation from the conditioning of the past, the traumas, resentments and emotional and mental states, in order to relax in the peace that is always there.

From 2001 till 2011, he has been an entrepreneur, hotel manager, consultant, lecturer and writer and has been hosting inspirational and transformational seminars, workshops and group and individual consultations around the world. Bava uses his rich life experience in various fields of action (management, leadership, art, education, NGO, spirituality, and Reiki) to give individuals a fresh look at life and work so that they can get out of everyday problems and rediscover life's passion.

In the summer of 2011, Ivan experienced a strong expansion of consciousness and knowledge, and at the end of 2011 he turned completely to his mission of elevating human consciousness and spreading the message of the innate ability of every individual to live successfully, happily and satisfactorily as the creator of his life in harmony with the rest of creation.

School of Awareness & Spiritual Mastery

This is a school of fundamental spiritual and life knowledge for conscious and fulfilled life on the planet Earth in accordance with the laws of the Universe and the Spirit. The aim of the school is to awaken every individual from oblivion and turn them from the self-centred to a conscious-minded way of life. The school operates in English, Croatian and Spanish languages.

The Course of Awakening is a semi-annual online course with direct and continuous guidance by Ivan Bava via web portals, video footage, internet conferences and live coverage that focuses on direct self-awareness and awakening from the dream of this world. Participants adopt the habits of the Higher Consciousness for everyday life, change mental concepts and beliefs, while at the same time accepting the illusion of what surrounds them. The awakened individual is the most valuable asset of society. This is the most complete online knowledge course available in the Croatian and Spanish language, which through 75 videos provides wisdom and practical application into daily life.

www.omniacademia.com
www.ivanbavcevic.com
www.ivanbava.com

The Center of Consciousness

The Center of Consciousness is a community of local centers in Croatia, Slovenia and other South-Slavic countries. Those are places of socialising and learning that belong to people irrespective of their race, religion, nationality, gender or any other characteristic so that each individual can realise his or her highest vision of life and the goal of knowing oneself.

We are a group of individuals who devoted their time to serving the society and raising awareness. The center was founded by Ivan Bavcevic Bava, with his associates and friends. Bava's spiritual and practical lifelong learning is completely open to all, and transmitted in a contemporary and understandable language with the message's universality.

The Center of Consciousness provides:
1. Half-day, one-day and weekend programs of awareness and self-development
2. School of Awareness and Spiritual Mastery programs
3. Visiting lectures and seminars of world lecturers, teachers and writers
4. Basic Breath meditation and different types of guided visualisations
5. Reiki seminars of the first, second, and master-teacher level
6. Group spiritual trips around the world

www.ivanbavcevic.com
www.centarsvijesti.com
www.ivanbava.com

OMNI Academia

OMNI Academia is an online place for life skills, practical knowledge, a joyful and entertaining approach to life and success at work. We gather professionals from various areas of human activity who directly communicate to students of all ages through our online courses and bring them knowledge, experience, talents, skills and techniques for developing in a particular area.

www.omniacademia.com

Social Media and Resources

All of Ivan Bava materials are available in English, Spanish and Croatian on YouTube, Facebook, Instagram and webpages.

instagram/Ivan Bavcevic

youtube.com/@IvanBavaOfficial

facebook.com/ivanbavaOA

www.linktr.ee/IvanBava

OA
MASTERCLASS